MARCH FOR OUR LIVES

MARCH FOR OUR LIVES!!!

MARCH
FOR OUR
LIVES

You're Either With Us or Against Us
Are You In or What???

by ELLIOTT LEW GRIFFIN

March For Our Lives
– You're Either With Us or Against Us

Copyright © 2019 Elliott Lew Griffin

ISBN: 978-1-0966-8305-6

Written by Elliott Lew Griffin

Cover Design & Text Formatting by: www.CrunchTime Graphics.com

Ordering Information: For details, contact the publisher at the above mailing or website address.

Scripture quotations marked KJV are credited to the King James Version, Public Domain.

Category: Social Science-Violence in Society |
Law-Government-Federal

Published & Printed in the USA

MARCH FOR OUR LIVES!!!

"Your either with us or against us"

Are you in or what???

Stand up!!!

And

March for OUR LIVES!!!

OMG!

A must read!!!

THIS BOOK IS WRITTEN TO ACKNOWLEDGE ALL THOSE AFFECTED

BY GUN VIOLENCE HERE IN AMERICA

AND AROUND THE GLOBE...

"I'M SORRY... WE FAILED YOU!"

THEY SAY:

"ALL IT TAKES FOR EVIL TO SUCCEED IS...

A FEW GOOD FOLKS WHO STAND BY AND DO NOTHING!"

-ORIGINAL AUTHOR UNKNOWN

HOWEVER... I'LL SAY:

"IF THE FEW GOOD FOLKS STOOD BY AND DID NOTHING...

THEN OBVIOUSLY THEY WEREN'T GOOD FOLKS AFTER ALL"

-ELLIOTT LEW GRIFFIN

SO THEREFORE... I'M ASKING:

ARE THE GOOD FOLKS GOING TO STAND BY AND LET EVIL WIN?

OR... ARE WE GOING TO STAND UP AND PUT IT TO ITS END...

"SHINE"

You, you threw my city away

You tore down the walls and opened up all the gates

You, you ruined this town

You burned all of the bridges, and you slowly let us

drown

But you're not gonna knock us down

We'll get back up again

You may have hurt us

But I promise we'll be stronger and

We're not gonna let you win

We're putting up a fight

You may have brought the dark

But together we will shine the light

And whoah, we will be something special

Whoah, we're gonna shine

We're, we're gonna stand tall

Gonna raise up our voices so we never, ever fall

We're done with all your little games

We're tired of hearing that we're too young to ever make

a change

'CAUSE YOU'RE NOT GONNA KNOCK US DOWN

WE'LL GET BACK UP AGAIN

YOU MAY HAVE HURT US

BUT I PROMISE WE'LL BE STRONGER AND

WE'RE NOT GONNA LET YOU WIN

WE'RE PUTTING UP A FIGHT

YOU MAY HAVE BROUGHT THE DARK

BUT TOGETHER WE WILL SHINE THE LIGHT

WHOAH, WE'RE GONNA SHINE

WE CAN HUG A LITTLE TIGHTER

WE CAN LOVE A LITTLE MORE

LAUGH A LITTLE HARDER

WE CAN STAND UP AND ROAR

IF WE ALL COME TOGETHER, IT WILL BE ALL RIGHT

STAND UP FOR ONE ANOTHER, AND WE'LL NEVER GIVE UP THE FIGHT

YOU'RE NOT GONNA KNOCK US DOWN

WE'LL GET BACK UP AGAIN

YOU MAY HAVE HURT US

BUT I PROMISE WE'LL BE STRONGER AND

WE'RE NOT GONNA LET YOU WIN

WE'RE PUTTING UP A FIGHT

You may have brought the dark

But together we will shine the light

You're not gonna knock us down

We'll get back up again

You may have hurt us

But I promise we'll be stronger and

We're not gonna let you win

We're putting up a fight

You may have brought the dark

But together we will shine the light, and

Whoah, we will be something special

Whoah, we will shine

-Sawyer Garrity and Andrea Pena

MSDHS

MARCH FOR OUR LIVES!!!

TABLE OF CONTENTS

MARCH FOR OUR LIVES!!!

GOD:
Please grant me the serenity...
To accept the things i cannot change,
Courage to change the things i can!
And wisdom to know the difference...

-Serenity Prayer

Alyssa Alhadeff

You know what? I've been looking for the words to start this book with ever since I decided to write it. And every time I tried to begin for the past week, my mind just drew a blank. Of course, I immediately thought action, but maybe I just needed a moment of silence to stop, think, analyze and process what I was experiencing myself. Cause really, what do you say in a moment like this... where you can't find the words to tell it like it is. I guess it's like the country song says, "Just close your eyes and let your heart lead the way, what do you say?" But still I'm left thinking where do I start? I know a journey of a thousand miles all begins with a single step, so with my first step, I would ask *Why???*

To be honest, it's not even a question of why Nikolas Cruz did this, cause to me, after hearing everything to date the warning signs of this troubled teen was there all along. And our local, state and federal government failed to act on the warning signs that would have prevented this horrific tragedy from ever occurring. That's why every time I begin to write again my thoughts just get mumbled – jumbled. So... I pause to wait on the right words to say or try to search for the right words to say. The more and more I think about it, the only way to say it is just to say it like it is... The truth shall set me free... so if I happen to get all over the place from time to time, please bear with me cause I hope to bring the message of this book to one consistent end and that is we literally have to...

MARCH FOR OUR LIVES!!!

For the past few weeks I have watched our government officials and members of the National Rifle Association (NRA) point fingers at everyone, but what they failed to realize is, as they were pointing a finger at everyone — three fingers were pointed back at them. Yes, this horrific tragedy of Marjory Stoneman Douglas High School (MSDHS) was perpetrated by none other than Nikolas Cruz. But, it was actually perpetuated by our own government and the NRA, too. That's why my first question is to them... and it's *"Why???"* *Why* would they continuously allow the sale of assault weapons knowing their only purpose is to kill humans? *Why* would they continuously allow the sale of large-capacity round magazines knowing their only purpose is to shoot as many people as possible? *Why* did they ever allow the NRA to sell bump stocks when they've known from day one that **this accessory turns a semi-automatic assault weapon into an illegal fully automatic machine gun?** *Why* would they ever allow the sale of a semi-automatic assault weapon to be sold to a 19-year-old teen when he couldn't even purchase a semi-automatic hand gun or a bottle of beer till the age of 21? Then, even if they were to change the gun purchasing age to 21, my question would still remain the same… *Why* would our federal government still allow the sale of assault weapons in the U.S.? Especially since they must know that mass shootings with these weapons went up 200% after the Clinton era assault weapons ban was lifted in 2004. Two-hundred percent and assault weapons are still allowed to be sold on our streets (both legally and illegally). It just doesn't make no sense to me! I may not be the sharpest tool in the drawer, but even the kid from MSDHS questioned: "*Why* does it take so many lives to be lost, so much blood to be spilled" before *We the People* can get our federal government who's sworn to protect us, to implement comprehensive gun reform laws. Laws that will keep kids safe in schools, the People safe in our communities and all of us safe around our nation. With all of these mass shootings going on here at home in America, *why* haven't they implemented stricter gun laws to date? And most importantly, as another MSDHS student questioned: "*Why* wasn't the first school shooting the last school shooting???"

Why? Why? WHY??? That's the question I want to know is "*Why*"? *Why* do these kids and the People have to March on Washington just to get our federal government to implement common-sense gun laws that will save lives? And *why* do they continuously allow the sale of firearms in our Country? They know beyond all possible doubt that the gun background check system currently in place… according to their own words… is severely flawed "and widely unvetted". The gun show loophole allow countless firearms (millions upon millions of guns) to fall into the hands of dangerous criminals and gang members like MS-13, bloods, crips, hoodlums, little street punks and even the KKK, from North America to South America and everywhere else in between.

The crazy part is our federal government knows all of this and have known all of this forever! So, to answer my own questions stated herein honestly, I would have to state, "THEY SIMPLY DON'T CARE", Period! Not only that, but the fact that they've known of this forever, and have done nothing behooves me. They have allowed all these dangerous criminals to get their hands on these guns that's killing and terrorizing people in our communities. And, still have refused to do anything about it. It's treasonous to us the American People. Especially since we now know that our very own President and several members of Congress are and have been getting paid to look the other way by the NRA. In wake of all of this madness, we now know that Trump himself received over 30 Million Dollars from the NRA for his presidential campaign alone. Over "THIRTY MILLION DOLLARS???" Then we also know that Senator Marco Rubio got over 3 Million dollars from the NRA in donations for his campaign. So, the question is... *How many other congressman and congresswoman received money from the NRA to turn a blind eye to all of this flawed background check system and gun show loophole madness?* Even after our very own elementary school kids were killed at Sandy Hook, they still didn't have the moral decency to fix the system then! Politicians and gun totting Americans constantly scream they want the Second Amendment and "don't take away our guns" but if they can't responsibly control who gets their hands on them (law-abiding citizens vs. dangerous criminals) then nobody should have the right to possess them. If the American Gun Corporations, the NRA and the law-abiding citizens of America can't come together and close all of the loopholes then *We the People* must! *We the People* must come together and close the entire hole until they decide to get it right and fix it permanently (i.e. meaning ban the sale of all firearms in the U.S. until the entire system is properly fixed and up and running.)

It's like Trumps travel ban. As soon as he became president, he instantly put in effect travel bans from several Muslim countries due to our inadequate vetting procedures in those areas. Trump claimed that the inadequate vetting procedures allowed dangerous terrorists to enter our country against the safety and security of the American People. After a judicial challenge to an amended travel ban, the courts ruled that it was constitutionally enacted, and parts of the travel ban went into effect. But here we have dangerous criminals and serial killer gang members, which is nothing less than a domestic terrorist, getting their hands on an unlimited supply of firearms from our many firearm loopholes here in America! Yet, Trumps not calling for a firearm ban to protect *We the People* and our kids from these domestic terrorists until our gun background check system is properly vetted and all of the gun show loopholes are permanently closed. Which for lack of screaming and hollering… Should be done… TODAY!

That's why I say they're paid off. *They must be.* Because they know millions of firearms are falling into the hands of these domestic terrorists. The very ones that have terrorized the entire continents of North and South America. Even into the hands of the Mexican drug lords and Columbian cartels. The whole entire Mexico and South America drug wars were proliferated by violent criminals using American made firearms and assault weapons. *Why???* Because President W. Bush and the then Republican Congress were paid by these gun lobbyist groups, like the NRA, not to renew the Clinton era assault weapon ban that went into effect in the U.S. in 1994. So… instead of renewing the assault weapons ban in 2004 and/or outright permanently banning them forever… the W. Bush Administration got paid off to allow these high-power weapons of war to hit our streets with unvetted procedures for the past 14 years. Which since then, mass shootings with these assault weapons have went up 200% here in America and probably even more south of the border.

Now we have Trump's dumbass (excuse my language) sitting here on Twitter and many of our crooked Congress members sitting on their hands, with their thumbs up you know where… while thousands upon thousands of assault weapons are still being sold out in our stores cause they've all but refused to reissue a ban on them. Not even to mention we still have dangerous domestic terrorists *still* out there purchasing thousands upon thousands of firearms at these idiotic gun shows cause our government officials *have not* done anything to close the loopholes and/or shore up the background checks, even after more of our kids got massacred at school. We aren't even half way through 2018 and how many school shootings have we had. (Google it). We are nowhere closer to banning the sale of assault weapons than we were yesterday. Domestic terrorists with criminal backgrounds are still allowed to purchase these weapons of war TODAY. I'm sorry, but am I missing something… or does all of this reek of corruption by our government officials?

Here, we have Robert Mueller investigating Russia for meddling in our elections for the past year cause they bought social media ads. Yet we all know that these Big Gun corporations and Pharmaceutical companies have been meddling in our elections for ever, yet where is the investigation into that? We have direct evidence out of the horse's mouth that our president and members of congress have been accepting money from these lobbyist groups for years and *We the People* can't get collusion or meddling in our elections for that? Like I said, even after the Sandy Hook Elementary School shooting the Democrat's tried to pass comprehensive gun reform measures, but it was members of the Republican party that wouldn't jump on board with it. And now the question is… *How many of them refused to jump on board because they were bought off not to do so?*

Now I have sat here and watched members of the Republican party blame the Democratic party for not implementing gun reform when Democrats held both the White House and majority in Congress under Obama. However, if they can sit there and say the Democrat's should have fixed the gun problem… then they've just admitted there is a problem and what's wrong with them fixing it now? That's what I care about! We can go into the should of's, could of's, would of's, but did nothing's all day. To me, that still doesn't get Trump and the Republican party off the hook. Especially since they've admitted that we have a problem. We also have them on record refusing to fix this crisis even after Sandy Hook. Just like they didn't want to outright ban bump stocks after the Las Vegas shooting. They knew way before that incident ever occurred that bump stocks turned a semi-automatic assault weapon into a fully automatic illegal killing machine,

Not to mention that they have known forever that the gun background check system was systematically flawed. And… they still didn't fix them after the massive church shootings in South Carolina and Texas and again after the Pulse Nightclub shooting in Orlando, Florida. That's why I started this book off with a question to them as to *why?* Cause really… *Why does our federal government continuously allow this to keep happening and do nothing about it?* Even after they swore under oath and on a Holy Bible to protect us. I guess that doesn't mean nothing to Trump cause he also took an oath and swore on the Holy Bible to uphold the U.S. Constitution and he lies to us every freaking day. Every time he opens up his mouth it's a lie. You see what he does… He even recently berated Hope Hicks for finally admitting that she tells little white lies for Trump, but nothing substantial though… Yet, she was the White

House Communications director in this Trump administration, (talking about FAKE NEWS huh?) Yeah sure, no wonder why they went through 5 White House Communication Director's in a little over a year because Trump fired them when they didn't want to lie for him no more, and/or resigned when they flat out refused to partake in all of Trump's conspiracies, to continuously lie to us, the American People. Yeah… Sorry… but nobody I know is buying this load of B.S. that the Trump administration is trying to sell us anymore. Even these kids at the MSDHS know that everything the government is saying is bunch of B.S. They even knew that the NRA bought off our politicians. It shocked the politicians so much that these kids knew, they immediately ran to the media outlets and began calling these kids crisis actors. Yeah, the cats so much out the bag that even the kids know and how sad is that? You know what, it just goes to show how out of touch our politicians are with reality. I mean just under 10 years ago they could get away with all of these backdoor lobbyist deals they had going on. But now, with the age of the internet, everything is readily available at our finger tips (it's over!). The kids these days are way smarter cause whatever they want to know they just google it and it pops right up on their phones since it's all public information. Now our politicians seem shocked to find out that all of their backdoor deals that they're use to doing, are now out in the open on the World Wide Web for the entire world to see.

The politicians have talked so much about us needing a special counsel for the Russia investigation, but really what we need is a special counsel right here at home in the U.S. to investigate all of our own politician's collusions with all these special interest lobbyist corporations. Not to mention we have private prisons cashing in on 2.2 Million People incarcerated. The U.S. has only 5% of the total world's population, and yet we astronomically hold 25% of the total number of the world's prisoner population. To say the least… there is something wrong with everything our government does and we all know everything is wrong with at least half of what they say!

The crazy part is our problem is not just on a federal level. The kids at MSDHS went to their Florida State Legislative Office in an attempt to get a ban on assault weapons just in their state. Their legislatures rejected a proposed ban on assault weapons and large-capacity round magazines in a 36-71 vote. To just hear the ban, I shook my head. Like the kids later said in TV interviews… "It was heartless how fast they pushed the button to say 'NO'…" You know what the astonishing fact that we found out was… that all these politicians that said 'NO' were all Republicans with an 'A to A+' rating as members with the NRA, except for like two with no rating and one with a 'D' rating. Then the guy with the 'D' rating was one of the few legislatures that stuck around in Tallahassee to answer these kids questions the next day. Like many of these kids said, their lawmakers "danced around our questions", "dismissed us, ignored us" and as one kid said, "To not even give their assault weapons ban a chance to be discussed, disgusts me". It was really sad to see how these student survivors in the wake of burying their friends, rode several hours on a bus to Tallahassee to meet with their politicians and were only left to be discouraged after this meeting with them.

But you know what, while they were very disappointed, I could see in their eyes they were not going to give up. Like one kid said, "we're so much more determined" another called out to the NRA stating, "we are not afraid of you". Another said he was "super-pissed" and that "we are so strong, we are so powerful" and I am going to say *they are!* I was so proud of these kids. Just to sit here and watch these teenagers speak from the heart, their emotion, their passion, their pain, their strength was heartfelt. They have called out for help when stating "how many people must die" and "help us so no one else dies" and *We the People*, as the adults of this country have to rise to the call.

You know what inspired me the most was when they said, "we don't even want your thoughts and prayers, we want action". That in and of itself was moving and when they shockingly discovered that their Florida State Legislature wasn't going to act on their behalf they even stated they were going to "get new representatives to represent us". I mean these kids were well spoken, articulate and extraordinary. Every time one spoke they were poised with great character and integrity to the point it was a complete disbelief to some of our politicians that these kids were smarter than them. To be honest just hearing their many speeches I was inspired by them and that's where I got all of this from, *Our Kids*. Their hope gives me hope, their determination gives me determination and their will to fight, keeps my will to fight alive. We will not be overcome, we will not be dismayed, and we will not be silenced. To those kids I would say keep it up and keep hope alive! At the end of the day we don't care what the NRA can live with. We know what we literally can live without... and that's these damn human killing war assault weapons and mechanically altered machine guns!!! Yeah, let's not forget the large-capacity round magazines. They too have no place in society as their only function is to make a gun more lethal and ultimately harm more of us.

I will tell you who else I am extremely proud of... cause when state and federal governments failed to respond appropriately, our very own Corporate America businesses stepped up big time in just stating, "We have heard you. The nation has heard you". nd not only have they taken on the NRA and members of the Republican party personally, but they have acted faster and more precisely then our government professionally. American corporations like Dick's Sporting Goods, our nation's largest sporting goods retailer stopped selling assault style rifles, high capacity magazines and raised the minimum purchasing age to buy a firearm to 21; in their Field and Stream Outlets as well. Other major corporations like Walmart, the nation's beloved "go to" store removed AR style rifles, air guns and toys from their website. They too will only sell the remaining selection of firearms to anyone over the age of 21.

To be honest, it is a crying shame, how a teen couldn't buy a bottle of beer or a semi-automatic handgun at age 19, but he could legally purchase a war style assault weapon. *What? Really? You mean...? Say that again...* Yes! Talk about making no sense. What is making sense is how several of our American companies have now cut ties with the NRA, now that's American! Our hotel chains like Best Western and Wyndham no longer affiliate with the NRA. Other corporations like Delta and United Airlines, Hertz and Enterprise, Met Life and Avis will no longer offer discounts for NRA members. Other American businesses like First National Bank, Allied Budget, Starken and National have also cut ties with the NRA. And I know there are a lot more that I just don't have right here, but I would like to say, "Thank You!!!" These are real American people joining in on a real American fight to stand up to our politicians and the NRA, so more people can make it home to their families at night. As the days, weeks and months go by I'm pretty sure we will see more companies jump aboard as our kids have called out and called on all lawmakers to refuse donations from the NRA until we get the necessary change we so desperately desire here in America.

While the NRA claims these corporations have presented a "shameful display of political and civil cowardice" (they should look in the mirror), especially since each of these companies have acted with an "honorable display of political and civil courage". I'll tell you what... They're not too much of cowards cause they stood up to the NRA and that's more than I can say about our President Trump and the majority of the Republican politicians who seem to have all chickened out in the face of the NRA! (Scary bustards!) For real, they are literally running around like chickens or better yet snakes with their heads chopped off, trying to see what Trump or their base wants them to do instead of doing what the majority of us – the American People – pay them to do. It's called… **The Right Thing!**

Well I know one thing for sure, Trumps a living embodiment of his famous speech… The one that he stole from Oscar Brown Jr.'s song "The Snake". We knew he was a snake before we took him in. I guess we can't complain now that he has come back to bite the majority of us in our butts, especially with the several thousand lies and misstatements he and his administration have made to date. I swear all of the lies he has told has to of violated some kind of oath of office by now. Maybe Hope Hicks will continuously do the right thing and finally tell it all! But then again, what more do we need to see, cause I honestly can't take no more. (Is it Morrrrre? Make it stop already, please!) But honestly, maybe, she will answer some of the questions she refused to answer before Congress. I'm pretty sure she has more information than she told. Seriously though, we need to hire a special prosecutor to look into how the NRA and lobbyist are bribing our politicians in the wake of the fact that we know beyond all reasonable doubt that most of our politicians are making rules on one hand and cashing in on the other. Either way if you ask me, our politicians are colluding with these lobbyists and essentially meddling in our elections.

In the end, we have to stop it all. So, we need to just…

MARCH FOR OUR LIVES!!!

"Never Again! NEVER Again!
NEVER AGAIN!"

-MSDHS

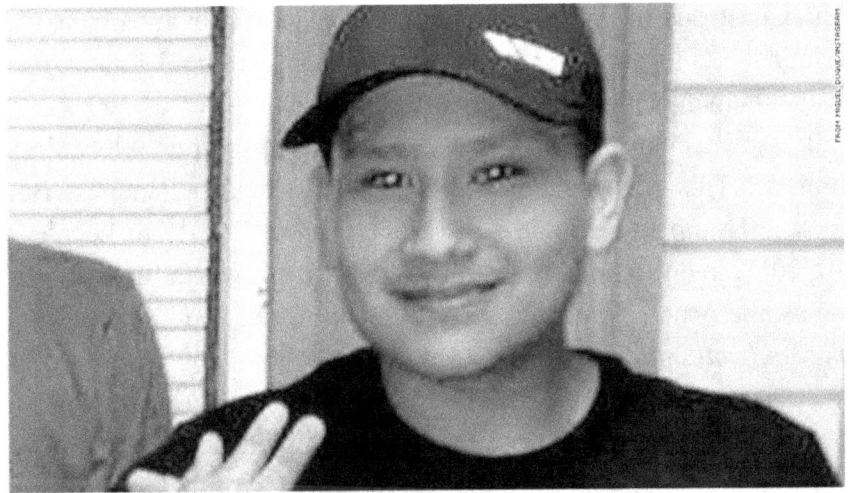

Martin Duque Anguiano

If we really intend to get to the point where we say NEVER AGAIN… we have got to really start changing laws and cracking down on gun show loopholes TODAY. I mean, let's face the facts… 91% of children struck by gun violence in schools is here in America. Of course, the root cause and common denominator of all shootings is guns. Now we're not just talking about a musket or a small rapid-fire gun that was around when the Second Amendment was ratified into our United States Constitution… People – we are talking about a semi-automatic to a fully automatic high-power combat assault rifle! So, surely things have changed since then… *right???*

Then we also have bump stocks that turn guns into fully automatic machine guns, extended clips that allow a person to shoot anywhere between 30-50 times without stopping. Not to mention, they have more than a 30-50% velocity increase over any musket or gun could fire during the time when the Second Amendment was written. Add that with the flawed background check system and the gun show loopholes, that's been around forever… Not to mention all of the assault weapons stolen from people every year. Now, we are up against one of the most dangerous cocktails known to man – a criminal… a lunatic… or a mentally ill deranged suicidal nutcase… with a human being killing war weapon machine… on a war path to kill as many innocent people as he can all before possibly killing himself! This was the Las Vegas shooter, Stephen Paddock. But look… Trump and Congress had from October 1, 2017 to February 14, 2018, to do something (anything) to try to prevent a future attack on us, the American people and our children, and you know what… *they did nothing!*

They could have easily banned the sale of bump stocks. Especially since they knew this device turned a semi-automatic weapon into a fully automatic machine gun, and/or they could have again easily banned the sale of large-capacity magazine clips. Both of which we know may not have prevented the Las Vegas Strip shooting, but more likely than not, would have prevented more casualties. And to be honest, this was the worst mass shooting in modern day United States history, where 58 people were killed and over 500 wounded. All of these innocent people… all they were trying to do is just have a fun night out at an enjoyable country music concert and got gunned down! Yeah, Trump claims that he's going to write-off bump stocks, cause they turn these weapons into machine guns, but he has instead sat on twitter… twittering… with his thumbs stuck up you know where… And every time he tweets, it's about something more and more dumb. All the while, Congress sits on their hands out of session every other week and here we are again... still talking about banning bump stocks and/or large-capacity round magazines cause they consistently kick the can down the road... on everything but their tax break that benefits who??? *Them!*

The crazy part is while the government is kicking the can down the road, over 70% of the American people want stricter gun laws. A lot of which are just plain old common-sense gun measures. Most American's are now looking at our Government with disbelief that these laws and measures weren't implemented or seriously enforced before. We have had a severe gang problem, a massive gun violence problem and now we freaking know why... Our government is being bought off by the NRA and these gun lobbyist corporations to turn a blind eye, so they can sell millions upon millions of weapons to criminal gang members. All due to a freaking gun show loophole and an inadequate background check system. (I'm telling you, it's time *We the People* stood up!)

I'm going to be honest, I thought all of these guns on our streets of America were sold on the black market or stolen out of people's homes. Come to find out... Our Government has not only been allowing this to occur, but now we know of several Gun Legislative Bills that they refused to pass that would have fixed the problems. These Bills would have closed the holes, yet they refused to do it. This is an outright conspiracy against us, the American People, by perpetuating it all.

Like I said already, it's not only a conspiracy... it's freaking Treason... against us... the American People. With these unvetted gun procedures they have allowed these fully automatic assault rifle war weapons to fall into the hands of drug lords down in Mexico and Here, in America (MS-13). All gangs, including the bloods, the crips and the KKK. Then most recently we even saw militia groups such as the Confederates and the Nazi's with war style assault rifles. I know a lot of people in our government might not want to admit it, but all you have to do is rewind the tape on the Charlottesville, Virginia incident and what do you see... Nazi's Marching in the streets of America chanting "Jews will not replace us!" or Confederates Marching down the street proudly waiving their confederate flag with what...? American made war style assault machine rifles strapped to their chest. And now, we don't even know if they were criminals or not cause our background check system is like our missile defense system (it don't work) and our gun show loophole has more holes in it than swiss cheese. I mean we really have to get serious on Trump and our Government! Especially since we now know that over 40% of all guns purchased at the gun shows are sold through a loophole with no background checks... whatsoever! So, bottom line is... any Joe Blow or crazy criminal serial killer can buy one. And really, that's all a gang member is. A crazy criminal serial killer or domestic terrorist that terrorizes the community with an unlimited supply of weapons of war that he was allowed to purchase legally... even though he was illegal as heck! All through these gun show loopholes that our government not only knows of... but has treasonously allowed to persist *for ever*, consistently!

Is that why 600,000 American people are getting kidnapped every year? Cause they allowed it to happen? Sex trafficking is at an all-time high in America... And once again... they know about it... and allow it to continue? Trump, Bill Clinton, Harvey Weinstein have all been accused of sexual misconduct that once again, they've known about for years, but continuously allowed to go unprosecuted? I mean, the list goes on and on and on and... The local, state and federal government were clearly informed several times that Nikolas Cruz was armed and going to conduct a mass school shooting and yet they allowed it to happen. I mean... Am I missing something... Did I fail to get a memo... or is our local, state, and federal government failing us so bad it's not even funny. It's to the point that 62% of People say that our President is not doing enough. The White House Press Secretary, Sarah Sanders, claims "there is not a quick and simple answer". Well how about banning the sale of all guns in the U.S. until we get a freaking answer! They put a travel ban in place cause the procedures were unvetted, so surely, they can put a gun ban in place that would pass constitutional muster until a proper vetting procedure is put in place. *"Hello?"*

Then the heck with what Sarah Sanders says when she states *there is no quick and simple answer...* It's called... "DO YOUR JOB!", but they don't want to upset their base which is what it's going to take to get the job done. In every aspect Trump has pointed the finger and/or looked for a scapegoat... his favorite is "The Obama Administration". The crazy part about it is the other day, I heard him say this has gone on for "a lot of administrations". Like – yeah, duh, we now know that, but the question remains... WHAT IS HE GOING TO DO? We still can't get a definite answer on that other than supporting a Bill that's already been in place. He's going to take care of Bump Stocks... Okay when? When the gun corporations sell the rest of their over stocked bump stocks off the shelves? I mean... Wow!... let's get real here! They probably have a discount on them if you're an NRA member with a sign that reads in small print... going out of stock or better yet... you better buy before Congress or the President bans the sale of them cause once their gone, their gone... Right? That's their mentality... What... the President is waiting for a signal from them? Probably... That's what he acts like. Congress too. That's why I say they are all in collusion, together. I mean, *What do you Think?*

I mean, the Mayor of Oakland took a lot of criticism for warning her public about ICE raids, but that's no worse than Trump warning the entire American population to buy their fully automatic machine gun accessories before he bans them. ...Oh yeah, don't forget to get your extended clips and if you're between the age of 18 to 20 you better buy your guns now... I mean... what happened to the fact that he said he wasn't going to warn the terrorists of what he was going to do? Yet he's been warning every domestic terrorist here in America that he's thinking about implementing stricter background checks and closing the gun show loopholes. How about doing it TODAY??? How about banning the sale of all guns and gun accessories TODAY until all of our safety procedures are implemented???

Now that's how you make a difference! Cause now it's on the NRA and these gun lobbyists to finally get it right if they want firearms to be sold to law-abiding citizens here in the U.S. It's that easy. No one's saying we want to get rid of the Second Amendment. But, we as the American People have a constitutional right to life, liberty and the pursuit of happiness! A seriously flawed or unvetted procedure that allows criminal gang members or mentally deranged people to have literally unlimited access to essentially what is a war weapon literally infringes on our due process right of the Fourteenth Amendment.

So, I'm Sorry... I would rather live my life with freedom in pursuit of happiness than to live in fear of a criminal gang member doing a drive by on my street with an AK-47 or AR-15 or... have some mentally deranged psycho-path shoot up a concert venue or worse yet... our beloved kids at school. You know when they say you've crossed the line... Trump and our Republican government (cause, yes, I'm blaming a lot of bought-off Republicans on this issue)..., the issue of guns and the Second Amendment, they go hand-in-hand. Now if we were talking about abortions and/or planned parenthood I would say Democrats. But, then even on that issue, I would say the Democrats at least send the power back to the people to choose. Here, the issue is guns and the American People have spoken. Over 70% support stricter gun laws and 97% support universal background checks. That means 97% of the American People also support the closing of the gun show loophole and the person to person Craigslist black market sales without proper vetting. Another statistic is 77% of Americans say Congress has not done enough to prevent mass shootings here in America. Especially since that same 77% say that this Marjory Stoneman Douglas High School Massacre could have been prevented.

What was essentially to be a day of love for these kids and their families on Valentine's Day, February 14, 2018, we now have what's been called the Valentine's Day Massacre, because our local, state and federal government is inept and incapable of doing their job. Trump and our government wants to blame these mass shootings on mental health issues. Sure, I admit that they were, but on that same token, they have completely defunded the mental health system. I even was watching on TV where the Naval Academy was handing out less than honorable discharges to our Iraq and Afghanistan Veterans that became severely mentally ill due to their tours in these ongoing wars. I mean the entire system is broken and it is up to us, *We the People*, the American public to fix it. Like the kids said… "We'll get somebody else to represent us…" But then, we're back to the question of *"Who can we trust **not** to get bought off or **not** willing to take a bribe to do so?"*

I mean, our President, Donald Trump, got 30 something million dollars from the NRA. Just look before he was president or before he accepted that 30 million dollars and that endorsement. We have him on tape stating that assault rifles should be permanently banned here in America. But TODAY it's a different story. Before he was all for raising the age limit to buy guns stating on tape …it doesn't make sense how you can't buy a hand gun until the age of 21, but you can buy semi-automatic assault rifles, with an extended clip... So, he surely knows… but I say again, TODAY it appears as if it's a different story. Obviously, someone must have gotten in his ear or pocket! I say pocket, *"What do you say?"* Look at other Senators, like Marco Rubio, who received 3.3 million dollars from the NRA. I'm pretty sure other Republicans like Mitch McConnell and House Speaker Paul Ryan have received the same amount… if not a lot more. If that's not bought off, then I don't know what is???

The Republican's all keep talking about this Democratic National Committee (DNC) and Hillary Clinton paid Russian dossier and all that hoopla and how they want heads to roll, but when they were to come together to vote on a simple but monumental issue… Universal Background Check Bill on all guns… after our Sandy Hook Elementary School kids were horrifically killed… these scumbags were bought off not to vote on it… and they know that! The whole world knows that. I sure know it!!! (Freaking Scumbags) *We the People* have to come together to fight for our God given right called LIFE!

These kids go up to Tallahassee to get the Florida State Legislature to ban the sale of all assault rifles and who says, 'NO!'… all the NRA bought off Republicans. That comes as no surprise after the so-called "FAKE NEWS" media dug up records that the Florida Republican Governor and Florida Republican Legislature gave massive tax incentives to the gun companies to manufacture none other than AK-47s and AR-15s in their state. Yup! Ak-47 and AR-15 assault rifles are manufactured in the State of Florida. So, I'm pretty sure that's why all the Florida Republican Legislature, but three, have an "A to A+" NRA rating. Yeah!... They are the ones that are fake… Then, no wonder why they were so quick to say 'NO' to even discussing the issue of banning assault rifles in the State of Florida. I bet you that if we pull up the records on each of the Florida Legislature members along with the Florida Governor, Rick Scott, they all received some kind of campaign money or donation and/or incentive from the NRA to say 'NO'! and essentially to continuing the manufacture of these war weapons meant only for killing humans in their state. Cause, let's be honest... an AK-47 and/or an AR-15 with an extended 30-round large magazine clip is not manufactured for hunting game. Its sole purpose for manufacture is for war – and sorry – but the sole purpose of combat war is to kill as many people as you can... and as fast as you can... and as long as you can, - period! Ask any war Vet, he'll confirm it.

I'm serious, they really think we're stupid cause they have been getting away with it for so long, but the age of social media and the internet has caught up with them. Everything that they used to do in the dark, in the back room is now done in the light and out in the open for the world to see. A little less than 10 years ago, they could still get away with it. Now we are onto them and what's finally starting to come to light is... how these gun lobbyists are spending tens to hundreds of millions of dollars to influence our elections and our politicians are colluding treasonously with them to do so. Just look at the recent report of Jared Kushner, who miraculously received over 500 billion dollars for his devilish 666 New York building after meeting in the Trump White House with investors. He's had no security clearance, no skills for his foreign White House position and has major business dealings all around the world... where everyone is seeking some kind of influence into our American Society. Therefore, I wasn't even surprised when the media said, "Four Countries were looking into how to manipulate Jared Kushner". It must have had a lot of truth to it cause the next day or two, the White House downgraded Kushner's top-security clearance in an effort to sweep this growing probe under the rug.

As more and more facts come to light, we find out that our democracy has really fallen to the wayside, and all of our politicians are in bed with these election influential lobbyists. It is disturbing and frightening to know that in our face, they try to cozy up to us, but behind our backs they're dirty dogs. What's the saying, "You lie down with dogs, you wake up with fleas…" Something like that. So, no wonder why I been here scratching my head non-stop on this one, I thought it was dandruff, who knew it was fleas… (Ha-ha) Maybe I should check my scalp for ticks, cause our politicians definitely have been sucking the blood right out of us!

You know what? I'm going to say this though, cause when your bought off like Trump is by the NRA (30 million and counting), you can't effectively play the role of the Commander-in-Chief. And when you have Congress in on the bribes too, they can't effectively play the role of a Legislature whose sole purpose is to make laws that align with the views of the American people and not the lining in their jacket, pants or purse pocket… (Yeah ma'am, we are onto the stash the cash in the bra spot as well) This is not a game, folks! Kids are dying while these politicians are voting with whoever is putting the most money in their pockets and not what's beneficial to the American People. This is evident to those who have been fronting them and the way they have been voting! Trust me, with 31 million dollars and the endorsement of the NRA, Trump's not going to buck up against them very much. For 31 million more, he's going to forget all about it. Just like when he got the first 31 million from the NRA and all of a sudden, his opinion changed on the banning of assault rifles. What a coincidence, or you know what… *What a nexus!*

Just like Trump's sexual assault/harassment case. First you have 13-14-15 women coming out accusing Trump of some kind of sexual misconduct. Then, you hear Trump on the Access Hollywood tape admitting that he has perpetrated this kind of misconduct in the past. Oh, again what a coincidence or better yet *'a nexus'* cause everything he admitted to on the Access Hollywood tape these women were asserting he did. And then, the right-wing media had the nerve to claim it was just locker room talk. Well, you know what, it would have been just locker room talk if these 13-14-15 women weren't asserting that he did, what he admitted he does. Point blank simple! It's just like the Harvey Weinstein's phone call tape. When the women asked Weinstein why he grabbed her breast yesterday… you know what… as soon as Harvey said, "because" he instantly admitted to sexually assaulting the girl, point blank period!!

Donald Trump always criticizes Jeff Sessions for his failure to probe into the Hillary Clinton case. Maybe with the last string of criticisms Sessions received from Trump, we can get him to probe into Trump's sexual assault case. Sessions said he was a man of honor and integrity… I am too, so hey, let's start the investigation TODAY. I'm serious… I'm tired of these people… they flip-flop on us all the time. What they need to do is really stop worrying about their bottom lines and start worrying about OUR freaking lives! *That's for real!*

We are seriously trying to come up with solutions to stop these mass shootings and every time we try to put an idea on the table, we find out that the NRA already bought it out from under us. This is a red flag alarming conspiracy and as soon as Mueller's done with this Russia investigation, what we all need to do is MARCH on Washington and demand that he be put in charge of investigating as to what extent the lobbyists are meddling in our elections with our politicians. We need to see if we can't Trump up some collusion or money laundering charges with our very own… sworn to protect us… Government officials. I bet you these kids have more honor, integrity, morals, values, and ideas than the people in Congress. Heck, these kids would have already passed and implemented a gun bill with overwhelming support by now and they are only in high school. Yet, we (the adults) sit here and wait for them to act. At least a majority of Americans are screaming… "We want stricter gun laws!", for how long now??? A decade???

You know what, NEVER AGAIN should a child have to endure the pain and suffering these kids have gone through. NEVER AGAIN should a parent have to worry about sending their kid to school and wonder if they're going to make it home that night. NEVER AGAIN should a parent have to bury their kid cause of a massacre that our Government should have prevented. So, with that said… We really need to get our heads out of the freaking sand, and our thumbs out of our behinds and say Never Again if really want to stand up and claim victory…

MARCH FOR OUR LIVES!!!

Your either with us or against us,
So, are you in or what???

-MSDHS

Scott Beigel

These massive shootings are happening too many times and it must be stopped. This has become yet another epidemic that's plaguing our nation. In this day and age, school shootings are more common than winning the freaking lottery. With the lottery someone would be lucky to win once or twice a month. With these school shootings, we have had 15-18+ in less than 2 months... 2 months. And I know I've talked a lot about Republicans, but this isn't about Democrat or Republican (I would have said this isn't about red or blue), but technically it is because our common goal must be... to keep these combat weapons out of the hands of the Blood and Crip gangs that are using these assault rifles to wage war and terror on our streets. We have students and staff that do not feel safe at school, who can blame them cause at this rate 18+ school shootings in 2018 alone is alarming. It's as if we are sending our kids to school to get slaughtered. Our kids are begging for us to take action, pleading *"Please... take action!"* All the while, our elected officials are still taking money to do the opposite, or worse... And excuse me here... but to turn a blind eye even to what a blind person knows exists.

For the life of me, I don't know why it's taking these kids, who are strong and courageous and/or these shootings to fix what they already know is broken. They claim it can't be fixed by changing gun laws alone... Well one thing for sure, we know it won't never get fixed if we don't change the gun laws we currently have on the floor! Believe me when you have the NRA spokesman admitting on record that the system for buying guns in America is severely flawed and have been forever... you know we have a serious problem on our hands. This has been going on way to long with way too many instances for the American People to turn a blind eye too. You know they have a saying that, "We all have to face the music sometimes..." and you know what, I'm glad to be part of the messenger that informs you that *TODAY IS THE DAY!!!* (I almost said, sad to be the messenger, but everyone wants to kill the messenger) But hey, if that's what it takes for me to do my part to get the message out (then hey) I'm going to tell you like the kids told the NRA: *"I'M NOT SCARED OF YOU!"*

Because at this point its whatever it takes to get these weapons of war off our streets, out of our communities and away from our schools. Like the MSDHS students professed: "Our students and staff did not die for nothing..." and "We got to do something, now!" This is not a left issue or a right issue, THIS IS A HUMAN ISSUE!

This is an American issue! This generation of our kids, whether we want to realize it or not has been terrorized by school shootings. One after another until MSDHS was the 18th school shooting of 2018 and that was by February 14, 2018, on Valentine's Day.

Young people are standing up and we *must* stand up with them. These are real kids fighting a real fight, all while our politicians keep lying down cowardly and saying... everything is going to be all right. Well, I'm here to tell you... *IT'S NOT!* And it hasn't been! And to be honest, it won't be as long as weapons of war are commercially available for sale in our streets, stores, online, gun shows or anywhere else they can be had. These students are amazing, bright, and articulate. I don't know about you, but my heart would be broken even more if we were to lose another one. That's why I said the time to choose is now! We have a 2018 campaign coming up and a real chance to get real, responsible people in office. People that will act in accordance with American humanity and not have their hands out to be greased by the NRA and Big Interest Groups that are counterintuitive.

The politicians we currently have swear they are going to act, but I honestly don't believe a word they say. I would say... I'll believe it when I see it... but I really don't have the patience to wait to see if they're going to do it. Like so many have said, if they didn't do it after the Sandy Hook Elementary School shooting in 2012, some 6 years ago, then what makes you think they are going to do something now, TODAY! Yeah, I heard it all before, same song and dance where our Government offers thoughts and prayers to the families and nothing changes. The next thing we're back to insanity (doing the same thing over and over and over) expecting different results until our hearts are broken again with another breaking news story. Like... how do we as people, find the strength to get over this one… You know what I found… *I can't!* This is the straw that just broke this camel's back.

Like they say, "It is the right of every American… Especially kids… to grow up in a safe community shielded from these kinds of horrific tragedies!" But, here we are… *we are nowhere* closer to ensuring our kids safety at schools than we were yesterday… just like *we are nowhere* closer to ensuring our own lives from the day of the Las Vegas Shooting…which happened cause *we are nowhere* closer to ensuring our safety from the Pulse Nightclub Shooting or Sandy Hook, Virginia Tech, Columbine, The Cleveland Elementary School in Stockton California, way back on January 30, 1989… or any other massive shooting in between cause *we are nowhere*… I don't know about you, but me, I'm tired of being *nowhere*.

Almost 30 years and it's the same old two-step… the people ask and the politicians duck… We have questions… they have no answers. At least Bill Clinton tried when he signed into law a ban on assault rifles on September 13, 1994. But leave it to the warmonger… Bush Jr… to re-allow the sales of these weapons of war on our streets… which unleashed the massacre's we see TODAY. Who I might add… also got us into these two Wars… both of which was due to a lack of information by our intelligence agencies… or once again… was for the all mighty dollar… cause who knows now!

You know what we really might have to take the "In God we Trust" off our American dollar… cause if money is the root of all evil… that's eroding our values, principles and moral standards here in America, then it definitely is in direct conflict with the religious aspect of it. Besides 'spins and half-truths' are all we are getting out of this Administration and the whole lot of politicians currently in office from A-Z. It's like what Don Lemons on CNN said, "A Half-truth is still a whole lie." And, I'm sorry, but it made perfect sense to me. Take it for what it is, the truth. To be honest, I just don't know why they don't tell the truth, cause to me, simply telling the truth is easier to remember, than (a Hope Hicks) little white lie. Don't worry, the spin is that wasn't Fake News, it was just little alternate facts from an erratic Trump Administration that obviously lives in an alternate universe!

I'm sorry… I just got beside myself and so worked up that I just want to berate Trump and our politicians to the fullest extreme. I wonder most of the time, "what universe are they really living in". Here on planet earth, we have real kids losing their lives while these adults are playing around! At this point everything should be on the table to stop gun violence. And with Trump and most of these Republicans, along with the NRA, hardly anything is. We have kids from Parkland, Florida and people from around the world begging Trump and Congress to do something, yet we are getting no sense of real accountability or responsibility from any of our politicians. When something needs to be done, they're like magicians… it's like abracadabra and all of a sudden, they don't hear… or better yet we look around and they have all but freaking disappeared.

Well I'll tell you what! They need to reappear and do something cause real lives are on the line if they haven't got the memo, especially since had they acted after Sandy Hook or better yet, the first school shooting, this horrific catastrophe could have totally been prevented. Yet, here we stand in the wake of another mass shooting school massacre down in Florida, where 14 students and 3 teachers, killed, and 15 others wounded. And here we stand… with no major gun measure control legislature from Trump… or our 'so called' Congress. I guess I am just fed up with the way our Government is ran or worse yet, the way our Government is getting paid off to not run it. Well you know what? We need to run ALL of our politicians and lobbyist out of Washington and just start all over from scratch! Then maybe we can actually make a difference. Like the kid from MSDHS said, *"We are going to be the difference!"* And you know what Kid… "I stand by you!" What's the song say, "Won't let nobody hurt you, I'll stand by you…' (Liberty Material) Trust and believe Kid, you have real adults in the think tank that's going to come up with a real strategy to end this madness. What they say… "We just got to set our marks far and set our perimeters wide so there will be no children left behind." Little do they know it, or hopefully a lot know, but these kids are rewriting history as they speak and trust and believe, when it's all said and done… we are going to be on the right side of history. Like the kids have said (And I second it), "We will not be silenced… Let us change the future and let us change it TODAY!" Let me tell you, for kids they have had some very powerful and profoundly moving words. It's actually been making the difference! If we ever did need crisis actors, they're it. They've got my vote!! Sorry… I told you in the beginning that sometimes I ramble, but just remember to bear with me. I really do think these kids are amazing the way they have stood up for themselves in the face of adversity. I wasn't kidding when I said they have my vote!

Like Nancy Pelosi recently said, "We need to bring everything to the floor and vote on it all… right now." And she is right! We seriously have to do more to protect our children and ourselves and if that's taking on the NRA, the Bloods, the Crips, the KKK, or any other group, then so be it. (Forever, it's on) Kid safety, school safety, and our safety is our very existence and our local, state and federal government needs to do more to keep us safer than collecting a paycheck and a handout under the table. It is never too late to start TODAY, and it would be our greatest hope that our actions in the present would thwart a plot against us tomorrow. The NRA and other lobbyist organizations have a stranglehold on our President and Congress. We have to pray that the one's they do have a hold on just tap out. However, I guess Trump just officially announced his 2020 Presidential bid for re-election. So... we are just going to have to vote him out, cause clearly, he doesn't know when to tap out. Maybe he'll never see how he's just tried to be a president to his base and not a president to *We the People*, the American people, his constituents. During his campaign he vowed and gave us his word that he would do the right thing. During his inauguration he took an oath, swore to protect us with his hand on the bible, pledged, promised and has only left many Americans with a broken heart that millions more knew would happen from the very start. Instead of pledging allegiance to the flag and the American people, he's obviously pledged allegiance to the NRA and lobbyists. Everything he says is a bunch of hot air. It doesn't matter how he spins it or slices and dices it cause at the end of the day it's still baloney. What'd he say, "If Congress don't ban bump stocks... I will". You know what... that just proved my point... he had the ultimate power to make the decision right then and there and again he refused to act like the presidential leader he's supposed to be... in the interest of us, *We the people!* The American People!!! Instead... he is scared of his base, the NRA and lobbyists and everyone else he's taken large amounts of money from. Not only is he scared of them, he continuously is looking for a scapegoat in Congress... all so he could have limited liability... instead of accountability... What they say, "Never send a boy to do a man's job!" (Yeah, I guess we should have known that when they said the Trump White House has turned into a daycare.) To say the least, it was predictable, but to watch our President and Congress... *under oath and on their honor neglect to act*... when businesses have done it with briskness is a complete and utter insult to me and my fellow Americans!

My only question at this point is... When did money override the tears in those kids and those parent's eyes, our freedom, and our valued American pride??? Land of the free and the home of the brave, but leave it to Trump, cause for him I guess, that's just not TODAY. I mean, we just had a mentally unstable evil boy with a legally purchased weapon of war walk into our kid's school with an obviously large duffle bag or a backpack that he was allowed to have, pull a fire alarm and our kids evacuation route led them straight to him to slaughter. Like the kids said after that, all they heard was gunshots, screams and cries. A school that was once filled with laughter and dreams, is now filled with heartache, pain, cries and screams. One kid said he's losing sleep, I believe another kid said something to the effect of chopper's now haunt him and siren's now stalk them, while other kids have expressed that they spent 4 hours in the closet crying and weeping – on their phones messaging goodbye to their loved ones, "I might never get to see you again", so pardon my French… but… *F** NO! We won't be silenced!* 'cause you know what… We will continuously…

MARCH FOR OUR LIVES!!!
ARE YOU WITH US
OR WHAT???

March for our lives! March for OUR LIVES!
MARCH FOR OUR LIVES!

-MSDHS

Nicholas-Dworet

This was not a drill, this March for our lives (a real March) in March was real. No longer can we sit on the sidelines and do nothing, the time for doing nothing is over. We got to stand up for our kids, stand up for ourselves and stand up for our lives, dignity and freedom. This March just wasn't about keeping schools safe or keeping guns out of our schools, it was about keeping weapons of war out of our communities and out of the hands of criminals. It was about making all of us safe and sound. We are in need of immediate action cause those in power have not taken action. We have corporate America doing what should have been done already. Yeah, sure, the NRA is a strong organization that has been established since 1871, but you know what... *We the people...* The American People... are stronger and have been established at least one-hundred years earlier in 1776 with the 'Declaration of Independence'. So... the NRA can take their money and shove it and go sit down somewhere, preferably in the back, PLEASE... all the wayyy in the back, scumbags!

Over the past weeks our kids have been saying "help us, listen to us, keep us safe" (There have been 18+ school shootings just this year.), and still... we have seen no relief in sight. I'm sorry... but a few stores not selling guns, where others still are... won't never fix the problem. Thank you, for real, but *let's get real!* I tell you what, I am proud to see that these corporations and businesses have a moral and ethical identity with the American people, where our President and politicians have not. It lets you know that there are still a lot of good people willing to fight the good fight. It's like what the Delta CEO told Georgia Republican lawmakers that voted to strip Delta of their jet fuel tax exemption after they joined in the fight by refusing to give NRA members discounts... In so many words the Delta CEO said, *"Our values are not for sale"*, AND I'll add... *Nor are they for rent*, scumbags!!! But you know what I love... he didn't back down, he didn't cower, and he sure the heck didn't fold... Like none other than AKA... our president... Donald Trump does. You know what else... If I ever fly... you best believe it will be with Delta, even if it costs a few cents more!!! That's pennies on the dollar for our values, pride and our people. I wish I could say the same thing about our so-called Billionaire president, who's moral and ethical values are still for sale, for rent, and possibly for trade. Someone also knows that Jared Kushner's are too, otherwise they would not have snatched his top security clearance either. Who invests in a 666 building anyway, that's just as bad as living on Elm Street.

You know what? I know a lot of people are wondering beyond the March, how do they join in on the fray, what can they do to stand up and do what's right. A lot of people have opened up their wallets, purses, or bra's and gave money, which money does help to get the word out, but what really counts is your votes at the ballot box come this next election cycle. A lot of people always ask, "How do we drain the swamp and get rid of these lowlife... bought off... scumbags? And you know what? I'll let you in on a little secret... if you want to get rid of all of them – don't vote for none of them. It's really that simple. Don't cast a single vote for anyone who is currently in office and jerking the people around and by the end of the year... they'll be gone!

We'll have a fresh new house and a fresh new senate. Come 2020, we don't cast a single vote for Trump and you know what??? We'll have a fresh new president! Yay!!! *We the People* have the ultimate power to vote these people in and *We the People* have the ultimate power to vote these people out! For real, our congress's approval rating is less than the age of a high school kid that attends MSDHS – 17%. (Lower than that, actually) At 60% they failed us and at 16%, they ought to be jailed, cause obviously, we know when we vote at these consensus polls, they aren't worth crap.

To be honest, I talk a lot about our federal legislatures, but I can't get over the 71 Republicans... in the Florida State Legislature... that voted 'NO!'... or the fact that they weren't even interested in discussing the issue these kids brought to their attention, for real. They wouldn't even consider taking up a debate to even talk about it... they flat out said 'NO!' with no remorse! *And literally did nothing.* I just couldn't believe how these people shot these kids down after they were just shot at and traumatized like that.

You know what… I'm really interested in how much money each of these 71 Republican Florida State House Legislatures received from the NRA??? Like these kids said crying, "Their votes were cold hearted". And you what another kid hit it right on the head when he said, "They weren't there, they don't know what it feels like to be hunted down, murdered in cold blood… They weren't there so they don't care!" Another one also said the truth when he said something to the effect of, "Their kids weren't there, so again they don't care"!!!

I mean, if these lawmakers were going to say 'NO' to these kids, they could have gotten on TV and said 'NO' before these kids got on the bus to go there. But, I'm so proud of those kids, cause they showed up and stated, "We're here to make a change". When they said 'NO', the kids said we are going to "vote them out and replace them with people that work for us!" It didn't stop there as these kids proudly stated, "We are not going to stop!... We are ready for action!" I'll tell you, these students poised with dignity have demanded some change and I'm proud to say… I'm demanding it with them!!! So again… *Are you with us or what???*

Like one kid said: "They think we are going to go away…" I'm going to finish off that statement and say, "Definitely not TODAY!" You know what, when does our politicians and government officials acceptance of bribe money to look the other way from the NRA turn into blood money. What do we have 26 innocent elementary school kids… first graders – second graders – third graders, killed in the Sandy Hook tragedy; 50 in the Orlando Pulse Night Club shooting; another 58 murdered in cold blood in the Las Vegas shooting with over 500 wounded… and now 17 more kids and teachers massacred at MSDHS and this is just the tip of the iceberg… We still had 787 people murdered by gun violence on the streets of Chicago just in 2016 alone; hundreds more… 650 people plus murdered by gun violence again in the streets of Chicago in 2017; and we haven't even made it to LA or New York. Let's not forget the church shooting in South Carolina, or the church shootings in Texas either. All the while, our congress and president knowing these facts… Columbine, Virginia Tech, U.C. Santa Barbara, San Bernardino, etc., etc… the freaking army base for crying out loud… and these people still refuse to act!!! They still refuse to close the gun show loopholes; they still refuse to implement a proper mental health, background check vetting system. And furthermore… they still refuse to ban these combat assault weapons of mass destruction. The very weapons that in most of these massacres have been the weapons of choice!!! Like the nice lady on CNN, Kirsten Powers, said, "It's these guns… that's when this problem started". It is the Bush Jr's Administration and the Republican party that were paid off by the NRA to lift the ban of these horrific assault rifles that have released terror, death, dismemberment and destruction on our streets since 2004.

Like she said, *"This debate is not about gun control, it's about gun violence!"* Our kids and our people, the American people… *We the people* are getting mowed down by these crazy lunatics on the day of Love – Valentine's Day and our very own, home-grown politicians won't even stand up to the NRA and say… NEVER AGAIN? Humph… Senator Marco Rubio even confirmed it at the CNN Town Hall meeting saying, "he won't stop taking money from the NRA…" How pathetic is that! And it's not, "What these kids are going to do…" It's, *What are we, THE ADULTS, going to do???* To me, these kids have already proved what they are going to do! They are going to stand up, speak out, and March for OUR LIVES…

Thousands of kids have already staged walk-outs across Florida. Western High School, High schoolers from Browand County – Miami – Dade County, students all across Florida walked out of school. Hundreds of shooting survivors rallied at the Florida

State Capital demanding nothing more than common-sense gun laws and still nothing. And what was just as troubling was while our politicians played politics; while our so-called president went on a Twitter tantrum sending out 21 tweets that weekend and played golf on President's Day… 2 of the slain MSDHS Students funerals were held nearby… What a president we have in Trump… I mean… a real stand up, take charge, kind of guy… Go Trump… *NOT!!!* I mean *REALLY????* You couldn't take the time to attend… Like my 5-year-old nephew says, "That's Disgusting!" Fox News always wants to know why Trump has such a god-awful low approval rating of 35% when the country's economy is doing so well… I just shake my head about how stupid they sound cause at the end of the day… All they care about is money… I give the GOP's credit cause they really care about their bottom lines, but that's why Trump has a 35% approval rating… cause he is busy pocketing the money instead of empathizing with our kids and saving all our freaking lives!

That's why we got to March for our lives… March for OUR LIVES… MARCH FOR OUR LIVES! Not just one time, not just one day, not just one month… Continually… until something is done! We have to March until the wrong is set right! It's time to act… now… TODAY, tomorrow, and for however long it takes! You know what, we will not fail cause *We the People* will not fail ourselves. We keep putting our faith in our elected officials when they obviously have no faith in God or in themselves. You would think that after all the Republican GOP lawmakers were involved in the Amtrak train collision with that dump truck, you would think they would have gotten a little humility, a little understanding, a little empathy. And that was after they sat up there at Trump's State of the Union address and did all of that B.S. clapping like they were holier than thou or did some Amazing service for the American People!

I mean… anybody could have come in and deregulated the entire system like they have… What did they do… As of January 31, 2018, the Trump administration has tried to kill 67 environmental regulations, some of them successfully. Their attitude is F** the environment. Global warming, according to them, is not real. Would someone please stand up and do the right thing. I mean, they say, "The tax payers are going to see more money in their paychecks?" *Yeah right!* And at who's expense… Yup, the taxpayers… Most Americans still don't even know if they're receiving a tax break or not, especially since millions are – for sure – set to receive a tax hike. Then according to the GOP's, the heck with the budget, their tax plan is set to pump 5.5 Trillion Dollars in credit into the U.S. economy and only get 4 Trillion Dollars back, thereby pocketing 1.5 Trillion Dollars. I mean, you do the math… 5.5 Trillion minus 4 Trillion equals 1.5 Trillion… in their pockets! So, please… listen to Nancy Pelosi. She's been around a block or two and knows that the few dollars that some (not many) Americans are receiving right now are the crumbs to the 1.5 Trillion Dollar Cake the GOP party is eating off of at this very moment! And if you listen to Paul Ryan, he tells it all without even meaning too. He's stated several times that "those bonus checks from these corporations are the result of the tax plan that we didn't even intend would happen". Meaning, in other words, they didn't even plan on giving you those crumbs out of the 1.5 Trillion Dollars they pocketed and to be honest, the only reason why some Americans got that was because of the honest and integrity of these corporations you see coming out against the NRA for the kids, you, and me. Otherwise, the American people wouldn't have even got that. And according to the records I saw… it was more like 4 Billion compared to 1.5 Trillion, so let's do the math… 1.5 Trillion minus 4 Billion equals 1.496 Trillion! So, when you look at it like that – how Nancy

Pelosi really sees it – the American people are getting crumbs compared to the 1.5 (even 1.4) Trillion Dollar Cake the GOP are eating off of. I mean we seriously have to sit down and get real. We can sit down and talk money all day long, but one thing for sure, money comes and money goes, but these kid's lives, our lives, everyone in America's lives is something we'll never be able to get back…something we'll never be able to replace… something we'll never be able to purchase… with all the money in the world. On that note, your kid's life, my life and your life are more valuable than all the money in the world you can muster.

I tell you, most people have seen death on TV, but when you see it in person like these kids have, up front, close and personal, their classmates, their friends, their teachers… you can begin to see why they are fighting so hard and why the tears are so real. This fight at the end of the day is not about money, cause at the end of the day money is just money. It really is a fight for our kids' lives, for our own lives. So, the next time we're at a concert, we don't get mowed down by the next deranged lunatic with a war weapon machine gun that our Government allowed him to purchase legally. Even though, it should have been illegal through an unvetted background check system or gun show freaking loophole. A system that even they've admitted has been severely flawed from day one. This is their words, not mine!

That's why we got to March for our lives… March for OUR LIVES… MARCH FOR OUR LIVES… and even if you don't physically March for our lives now, the real March is going to be in November of 2018, when we are all going to have to March down to the voting blocks and cast our ballots. I already told you the secret to getting rid of all of them – again it's really simple – Just don't vote for none of them.

Don't be pressured to quickly cast your vote. (Google their names.) Yeah, Paul Ryan, Mitch McConnell (Don't vote for them either.) And... I might take a lot of heat for this, but here's why... When we watched the State of the Union address, some of the Republicans are right... the democrats along with several members from the black caucus sat on their hands when they were supposed to be proud of a few of our accomplishments as a nation. The kid putting flags on graves; Black and Hispanic unemployment at a lower point in history, wages are going up. I mean, to be fair not only did it appear that they were obstructionists, but at times, it was disheartening to watch. I mean the Republican's did put it on thick, but I was expecting a little more thicker skin, so to speak, out of the Democrats. Put it this way... to not clap at the good points – the clappable points (come on help me out here), made it seem like they had no hand in our nation reaching those good points.

I don't know, to me, I give credit where credit is due and if it's not then I don't. What I'm saying is... At some point, we are going to have to suck up our pride and work together with the other side. Sure, Trump won. Whether we like it or not, he's our President until 2020 (or we impeach him, whatever comes first). I seriously doubt that there is collusion with "Trump" and "Russia", now Donald Jr. and Kushner (yes), they might be in for it. If anything, I would say Trump is colluding more with the NRA than Russia. And Obstruction of Justice with Comey admitting to leaking evidence with no tapes on what was said in the meeting is (let's keep it real) very weak. We might can get more out of his Access Hollywood Tape and sexual assault investigation than Obstruction. Sorry, just keeping it real. But let's be honest... come 2020 Trumps gone... He's one and done.

The only real reason Trump is even in there is because of Billary (Hillary and Bill Clinton), who both really did a lot. Come on, you can't say Bill Clinton without Monica Lewinsky coming to mind. And, he was one of two presidents to ever be impeached, even though both presidents, Clinton and Johnson, were acquitted in the Senate and therefore served out their term. (You thought I was going to say Nixon, huh! Nixon was disgraced and resigned right before he was impeached.) The Clintons… Bill kept lying to all of us, right to our faces. One lie, he said he hit it but didn't inhale… another one, he did not have sexual relations with that woman – I mean on and on and on. Yes, he did ban assault rifles in 1994, but enacted the AEDPA in 1996. And then there is Hillary's emails, which the Trump and Russia collusion debacle is all about TODAY… (those darn emails). We have Trump! (Wow! is definitely right)

Look, to be honest, I don't care about a Trump presidency past the extent that he is a moron AND a 13-time sexual assault/harassment loser. I don't care about a Hillary Clinton campaign past the extent that she, more likely than not, should of went to jail for negligence if not obstruction for her partake in this ridiculous email scandal. I honestly don't care about democrat or republican – or this I win, you lose mentality that I've watched played out over these past *several* administrations. Right now… all I care about is these kids… your kids – my kids… your life – my life. I just care about getting the guns off our streets, out of the hands of criminal domestic terrorists and out of the hands of these mentally deranged maniac's. Maniac's that quite frankly, have expressed no other interest than to mow you down – mow me down – mow our kids down. They haven't thought one bit to even stop and care about whether you or I am an Independent, or a Democrat or a freaking Republican, or a Socialist, or of the Green Tea Party… they haven't cared if their victims were Black, or White, or Hispanic, or Asian, or Indian, or Other… they sure don't care if your male or female… *They simply do not care!* We can sit right here and fuss and cuss and fight all we want to, but those bullets don't have nothing being identified to them. Their only objective has been to kill all of us or as many as possible.

It just so happens that the Republicans are in charge right now and yes, I would agree that they are bought off. So... as I see it... we are down to a few viable options. 1)We do nothing but pray it don't happen again. Hey, *Prayer is a viable option.* 2) We March our asses off like these kids are saying. We March, and we demand change, no matter whether you're Republican or Democrat. Hey – you got to mend the fences for the kids and our own lives sometime. See, this is what I'm talking about when I was referring to the State of the Union Address, but now it's the Republican's that want to sit on their hands when it's time to stand up and partake – (Just throwing that out there as a little food for thought) and 3) (what I see as our third and final option), We go to the courts and request a gun-sale ban like Trump's travel ban based on National Security reasons. The Republicans of the NRA are going to cry, but hey... a 9th Circuit District Court Judge would rule in our favor. It would pass constitutional muster, especially since, even the NRA has already admitted the background check system and gun show loopholes are drastically flawed and have been forever. Cause at this point, any Joe Blow criminal can still get their hands on a fully automatic bump stock assault machine gun which is a national security issue. Not to mention the U.S. Supreme Court already ruled that the right to own any gun is not unlimited. Sawed-off shotguns are not permitted, I don't see how combat assault rifles under the spirit of the Second Amendment should be either.

Sure, the Second Amendment says that the people are to match the militia to a certain extent. But, now that we have bomber planes and war drones, it doesn't mean that their commercially for sale to the American public and I don't see Army tanks sitting in everyone's driveways… The point is just because we have them doesn't mean that people have an alienated right to possess them (Just saying…). We do have options, but in the end, we need to band together like real Americans… you know *We the People*… cause they are the terrorists and we are the people, they are the hunters and we are the hunted – no matter what party affiliation, ethnicity, or age. Believe me, it's not about taking away no one's Constitutional right to keep and bear arms of the Second Amendment. Looking on the other side of the coin… having these types of arms is actually violating someone's life, liberty and/or pursuit of happiness and their due process right to the Fourteenth Amendment. You know, the one that makes sure that no one's Constitutional rights are being infringed upon. So, without further ado, I'm going to keep saying March for our lives… March for OUR LIVES… MARCH FOR OUR LIVES… cause the next life we possibly lose may very well be *your kids* or your own. I pray not, but school shootings, seriously, are more common than winning the lottery right now. Even if you have to bend a little for us to mend, one thing is for sure… we all need to be screaming for everyone's sake and…

MARCH FOR OUR LIVES!!!

*An ounce of prevention
is worth a pound of cure!!!*

-Benjamin Franklin

Aaron Feis

For the past few weeks, months, years, all we've heard from Trump, Congress and the NRA is "changing gun laws won't work". Well, will somebody please tell them that an ounce of prevention is worth a pound of cure! What our government officials need to do is stop taking NRA change and start making some freaking *real change*.

The NRA even takes it a step further when claiming, "in order to stop a bad gun with a gun, you need a good guy with a gun". But, will somebody again please tell them that the first thing we got to do is shore up our background vetting procedures and close the freaking gun show loopholes, so we can at least TRY to prevent the bad guy from getting the gun in the first place. Then we might not have to worry about putting our good guy's life on the line. If we can put our good foot first and do what needs to be done to prevent it before it happens.

The key is to stop the bad guy from getting the gun in the first place. There are a lot of procedures we can put into place that will prevent these bad guys from getting their hands on these weapons of war. I mean they've talked a lot about raising the minimum age to 21 in order to purchase a gun. But even then, if we look at the psychologist reports they tell us that an adult males neurological impulse control system in their brains aren't fully developed till the age of 25. So... we are still asking for trouble by allowing a 21-year-old to purchase a semi-automatic assault rifle. It's just that simple. That's why you can't rent a car until the age of 25, because the car rental companies know this fact.

We have spent a lot of time talking about the mental health issue. By legally selling a semi-firearm to anyone under the age of 25 is a mental health issue in of itself, because the impulsivity part of the brain is not fully developed. I mean let's get real, youth under the age of 25 have a lack of maturity and an underdeveloped sense of responsibility. This leads to recklessness, impulsivity, and heedless risk-taking. They are more vulnerable to negative influences and outside pressures, including from their family and peers. They have limited control over their own environment and may lack the ability to extricate themselves from horrific, crime producing settings. Their character certainly is not as well-formed as a fully developed adult. And, the immaturity, recklessness, and impetuosity makes them less likely to consider potential punishment. (Such as a mass massacre of this magnitude.)

There are really a lot of significant risk factors that we must really assess when it comes to selling youth firearms. Sure, if they want to drink alcohol at the age of 21, its allowable. But, let's look at youth death's due to drinking and driving irresponsibly. Everyone wants to view mental health as an intellectual disability or a mental issue of some form of depression or PTSD. Really, it's still a mental health issue when a person's brain is not fully developed yet. In most mental health that groups I've attended, we have talked of recognizing a high-risk situation. Allowing any person to purchase a semi-automatic firearm that fires in rapid successions without having to reload must be looked upon as a high-risk situation. Again, that's why most car companies require a person to be at least 25 years of age before renting them a car. Simply cause the risk of things that could possibly go wrong are overwhelmingly a lot higher. Just like selling a semi-automatic firearm to a person under the age of 25, who's brain is not fully developed yet is clearly an unreasonable high-risk situation to public safety.

See, the NRA opposes raising the age limit from 18 to 21 in terms of purchasing guns. Their focus is only centered on money. But our focus… Our focus must be centered on Public Safety, your kids safety – my kids safety, your safety – my safety. While the NRA opposes raising the age limit, as most Republicans probably do as well, **"It is Our alienate right, as the People of the United States of America, to determine what age limit is appropriate!"** To be fair… And to be clear… I mean, we just raised the age limit for buying cigarettes from 18 to 21. *Why* can't we raise the age limit on guns? Now, I'm not opposed to selling a 3-shot pump shotgun or a 6-shot revolver or a 7-shot handgun to a 21-year-old for home self-defense, cause I lived on my own around that age, so I know. But, when it comes to a semi-automatic rifle which comes in over 200 varieties, we might have to put our foot down as parents and tell our kids to wait a little longer, especially since, we all know that with age comes wisdom. That's why we developed a lot of age limits, from drinking to driving to smoking, in order to protect not only our kids but ourselves as well. Therefore, in considering mental health related issues, we must give great weight to not only the known mental health diagnoses, but we must also take into account the hallmark features of youth. We must consider the characteristics of adolescence as well as the diminished capacity of their neurological development which psychologist have determined don't fully develop till the age of 25. There is simply no reason... no reason at all... to rush to get our kids or ourselves killed.

We must first remember that the ownership of a firearm comes with great responsibility just as driving a car does. That's why we have laws put in place where you can't drive with a higher blood alcohol content than 0.08 percent; which we should put our foot down and say zero, but okay. *Why?* Because people's lives are on the line. That's why we have speed limits, cause driving too fast is an erratic behavior that more likely than not will lead to an accident. So, ultimately when we're talking about gun ownership, we need to set in place a higher set of rules to ensure our safety.

That's why they have a driver's tests. Every person must pass a driver's test in order to get a driver's license to be able to drive. *Why?* Because, we want to ensure that they know how to fully operate the vehicle and its functions before we allow them to get behind the wheel. And you want to know *why?* Because its safety first, plain and simple. Here we are... we sell a kid a firearm with hopes that he knows how to shoot it. We don't even know if he knows how to properly handle it, store it or even work it. We haven't required any classes, no training and/or taught them no safety requirement. Even our Police officers, who are trained specialists in weaponry, still must conduct quarterly training in order to properly ensure that their use of that firearm is in accordance with a standard of excellence. By selling a person a gun without even requiring a background check or a mental health evaluation has diminished our own American standards of human decency.

It's not that we are bad people, we just have to hone in on our standards of living and/or value of life, which like I said earlier, is priceless. Somebody shoot you – I can't buy another you... So, we must find a standard that will hold everyone accountable and to be honest... it's whatever it takes. That's why they have the saying that *an ounce of prevention is worth a pound of cure.* Ben Franklin coined it and I know it's true. Earlier I spoke of speed limits for driving to ensure our safety, but we also have other preventable measures that are in place that we enforce in order to save lives, such as seatbelts. A lot of cars now come with standard airbags; we have re-enforced vehicles; there are safety auto-stopping vehicles, and numerous other safety features, all this in case of a collision. I mean we have a lot of safety measures. When to use your low beams and high beams, when to change lanes, when to use your signals, how to use your mirrors. We have even taught our kids to look over their shoulders before switching lanes because objects in the mirrors are closer than they appear.

For gun safety, we don't have none of it. We don't even require a person to have a license to own a firearm as long as Joe Blow or Jane Doe can go to these gun shows and purchase a firearm with obviously no requirements. Phrased the way the gun purchase system is set up, it's basically like allowing a person to drive a car with no rules whatsoever. You know how many accidents we would have on our roads if we relaxed all of our driving regulations... It would be chaotic to say the least. People driving at high speeds – with no license – no insurance – drinking and driving – texting and driving – not wearing their seatbelts... You name it! I mean literally... how much of that do we see with police still ticketing people, even though we have had these laws in place for quite some time. I mean, you drive 80 in a 40 zone and see what happens.

All I'm saying is… we really need to broaden our way of thinking when it comes to gun safety here in America – or else gun violence will never stop. Ten years from now… we'll still be sitting here saying March For Our Lives, but still be in the same predicament we are in right now. The Columbine massacre happened April 20, 1999, and really… what has changed since then. The system is still broke. At this point, we don't even have common-sense gun laws on the books. We have a gun show loophole that's really ludicrous. Then we have the NRA and our politicians side-stepping and talking a bunch of gibberish about a Constitutional right to a Second Amendment that they don't even enforce the constitutional regulations of. I mean, they don't even want to raise the minimum purchasing age, or stop the sale of bump stocks, or limit the size of magazine capacity, or ensure that there is a proper vetting system in place that would prevent a criminal from obtaining a firearm.

The crazy part is Congress and past Administrations have had Bills on the floor that would have enforced some of these measures. And let's be honest… the Republicans have refused to sign onto them. The most notable one was presented in the wake of Sandy Hook and the Republican Congress still refused to jump on board. The bizarre part is we know why… because they really have been bought off not to do so. To be honest… *I see no other reasonable explanation for their failure.*

That's why I said they need to stop taking NRA change and start making some freaking real change, cause the days of getting paid to turn a blind eye is over. More and more everyday Americans are starting to catch onto their scheme of getting paid to look the other way and/or getting paid to do nothing. I mean, when I look at these kids, I can honestly say that our high schoolers are acting like leaders... and our leaders are acting like they're in a freaking day care center. They are acting so much like kids that our Intel Committee have built or are going to build a wall in between each other (the Democrats and the Republicans) due to a lack of trust amongst each other. Like... Okay??? And these are supposed to be the adults of this country that's going to lead us to great health, wealth and prosperity??? *Yeah right!!!*

I seriously think not! I don't know about you... but I have no confidence in our President or Congress to do anything worthwhile, let alone gun control. We can't even get them to make common-sense gun laws that an overwhelming majority of Americans would say make sense. To be honest, I have come to find out that they have no sense what-so-ever. It seems that their only objective as politicians is to sell us out for whoever's offering the most cents. I'm sorry... but that's the sense I'm getting out of all of this nonsense... *What about you???* This is why I applaud big GOP donors like Al Hoffman for stepping up to the plate and stating, "No more checks until the Republicans tackle guns". And in that interview, he said he called on all of his Republican friends to do the same, because he even knows this is a Republican issue. Let's be frank, the Democrats can't do nothing on gun safety measures without some support from the Republicans and it just hasn't come to pass. And I'm Sorry... I just can't come to grips with *why???*... Especially since, Congress has done literally nothing... even after our beloved elementary kids were murdered in the New Town massacre.

To me, this is just not fathomable! I don't know about you, but I am seriously flabbergasted at how incompetent and feeble-minded our Government really is. To say the least, it is just far-fetched to see how far off the mark the Republicans are... How out of touch with their constituents the Republicans really are... How extremely against, I mean heel-dug-in against, gun changes the Republicans are. *Really???* When we have our kids getting gunned down in our schools and on our streets??? Innocent lives are being lost and the Republicans are still catering to their donors on this issue. They instead should be catering to the safety and well-being of OUR lives. They keep saying they're going to act, but their words have just been idle words. Nothing has been put in drive. If anything, they have gone in reverse. With Trump, we have seen him back track on SOOO many issues from the DACA kid's immigration to now, on gun legislation.

To be honest on gun legislation, we are not even asking for a favor. All *We the People* are really asking for... is for our gun laws to be feasibly fixed. Plain and simple! And Trump and the Republicans are still acting like Freaking Flakes. I mean, we haven't even been able to get them (the Republicans) on board to stop people with felony's from obtaining restricted firearms. I don't know about you... but I'm fed up with the whole ordeal and for that reason... we really should oust these people come this next mid-term election cycle. Like I say, to get rid of ALL of them, all we have to do is don't cast a single vote for none of them. That's how you roll the dice and if you want to drain the swamp, then that's how you do it folks... you just pull the plug. Everything that has gone wrong has been on a lot of the Congressmen and Congresswomen's watch. We have two wars going that they don't have no clue of how to stop. Let's be frank and see the overall picture of how they can't even adequately control guns here at home, let alone control guns abroad. And go figure, they seriously just don't know what they're doing. They can't even stop the in-house fighting amongst themselves. They want to build a freaking wall in between each other and this isn't even a figment of my imagination, this is god-awful reality of these fools we have in our government.

I'm Sorry… sometimes I just go on a rant cause I'm tired of these politician rats constantly scurrying to get the cheese. I swear we need to lay out some mousetraps. The crazy part is they're not even scared to take the money cause there is no accountability for their actions. They are free to sell us out however they choose and to the highest bidder that chooses them. The more I sit here and think about it, the more I see how our government is so dysfunctional that it's disheartening. I've never been the one to be feint at heart but, listening to- and working through all of this crapola has just left me fatigued. This entire mess is a farce and a sham, and they know it. No wonder why Trump said, "he likes chaos" cause it's just meant to confuse us so we will give up. But, it's like these kids said, *"We will not stop!"* and *"Our friends and our teachers did not die for nothing!"* When you hear empowering words like that it makes you just want to turn on the accelerator. Cause… We are not giving up… We are not going to give in… We are going to put our money where our mouth is and do something about our problem. And the problem is gun violence, the equation is how to end it and the sum is Never Again. How do we do that? Everybody stand up and…

MARCH FOR OUR LIVES!!!

MARCH FOR OUR LIVES!!!

Ban assault weaponry
And change gun laws now!!!

Jaime Guttenberg

Y ou know what... I'm sorry... I just had to close that last
Chapter and collect my thoughts. I had a lot more to say on
preventive measures, but I got so mad at why they're not
already in place, it made me lose my whole train of thought and start
berating people. However, berating people don't work and really it
only makes things worse, but it makes me feel better, so I'm sorry.
I just get frustrated at most of the things our government do and
don't do that every time I look up... it's like really??? Are you
serious??? and/or just flat out calling them "idiots". OMG... I can't
believe it! To be honest I have those moments all the time and I've
learned that with Trump you just got to brace yourself cause that
point can come at a moment's notice. (i.e. a tweet or a bomb shell...

Hope Hicks fired for telling little white lies, or it's more breaking news of Trump's trade wars upsetting the entire world or the recent firing of Rex Tillerson, etc.) I'm pretty sure you get my point! Just everything about everything about this administration is ridiculous and it's just been unimaginable to see that they really don't know jack-doodly-squat. At times you just want to turn your back on them or wash your hands with them. But as soon as you start to turn your back or reach for the soap you're hit with the reality that *'It'*, no matter how preposterous, *'It'* still has an effect on my life. And, if I don't do something about *'It'* now, then more likely than not *'It'* will get more drastic later. *'It'* always does.

Especially when you look at these kids, or my daughters, I realize that I have to be the adult doer here. I have to be the worker and most importantly I have to act now! The time for not lifting a finger and/or not wanting to raise my hand is over. Now, I got to stand up and be accounted for and also be accountable. Especially since everything our president or government does is illogical. At this point, I'm still trying to iron out all the wrinkles in my life, but I'm up for the challenge. Sometimes I just got to absorb the blow a little more than I'm used to and try to do my best after that. Believe me this book wasn't as easy to come up with as one may think and trying to make a deadline to get it to print was a lot harder than it seems, but if your reading this, then I made it. For that reason, I'm proud of myself and I hope for some reason or another you are too. Maybe when you finish reading this book it will be a sense of accomplishment or maybe just hours out of your life that you can't get back, but just know that in the end… we all have the strength to overcome any obstacle that stands in our way, and what's standing in our way right now is Trump and Congress getting us *comprehensive gun reform* TODAY! So, whatever *'It'* takes to get *'It'* through, that's what we must do, but like the country song says: Just give me five more minutes.

Okay, I'm ready... I just took about 5 more minutes (Ha-ha)! You thought I wrote this all in one sitting, yeah that would be the day. This has really been a process, a lot of processing the information and then digesting how I feel about it. Then of course it's back to what I'm going to do about it and I just sprang into action and this is what I came up with so far... It's like Wow... Can I get 5 more minutes? What they say, can't resign, can't leave, can't quit now, so I guess we are stuck in between a rock and a hard spot. It's like the saying goes "you back the cat into the corner and somebody is going to get scratched," With this gun control issue our government has literally backed us into the corner by constantly refusing to do something about it, so we unfortunately have to crawl our way out of it. I don't know about you, but I 'm starting to grow my wolverine claws and I hope that you are too because this is going to be one heck of a fight.

The kids say March for our lives, but really, we are in a dog fight and *We the People* are the one cat in the corner. I would say it's a good thing we have nine lives, but this is not a funny situation cause in actuality... we don't. To be honest, if we don't act now, then by tomorrow somebody will lose their life again and it may have been preventable if we acted TODAY. So... to sit back and do nothing would be insanity! At this rate it's not a matter of who, it's a matter of when and therefore our actions on this issue must speak louder than words.

The only part of it is "action without thought is like shooting without aim". To make a long story short we have to know what we want? To expect our lawmakers to act on our behalf when we know they are bought off is like asking them to do nothing. I think that if we are demanding our government to act, then we must give them our demands to act upon and demand that they carry them out accordingly to our standards. Kind of like an ultimatum *change this, or we'll change you and get somebody in there that will do it*, period! There is no in between, there is no grey area, there is no wiggle room or even no room for compromising, and most definitely no if's, and's or but's. We want this or else! Or… we will oust you, *for real though…*

I honestly believe we are going to get something, but while something is something, something is still not good enough. I know it's better to "light one candle, than to curse the darkness", but if we light the candle and a gust of wind comes and blows it out, we are still in the dark every time. Basically, this is what the government is trying to do to us with their plan on fixing our gun epidemic problem here in America. In other words, if we have water spewing out of several holes in our dam, to just plug one hole would be needless and may only lead to other holes becoming bigger. What we have to do is go in and plug every hole in the dam in order to stop the water from leaking, period. If our government don't want to do that for whatever reason, then I'm sorry to say, that we got the wrong People for the job and we need to get People in there that can do the job.

So again, in order to stop our gun violence problem, we have to go in there and first get these heinous war weapons off our streets cause they have no penological purpose in our society than for killing people. Then we have to plug all the gun show loopholes, shore up our background vetting procedures, and then implement common-sense gun laws after that. I know I heard Nancy Pelosi say that what Congress does is allow a bill to get so big that People get hung up on a part or two of it and essentially, they don't want to vote for it for this minute reason. I get that, so what I'm proposing they do is just do one issue, one bill at a time. In other words, light one candle at a time until we get the room fully lit. If it was up to me I would say shut off the water (i.e. Temporarily stop the sale, transfer and trade of ALL firearms in the U.S. and fix all the loopholes and laws including Craig's List.) Similar to what Trump did with his travel ban. Then fix everything one by one. This is one gun show loophole and this is what we are going to do to fix it. This is another gun show loophole and this is what we are going to do to fix it.

It would even be better to do one issue on one bill at a time because let's say that one of our solutions isn't working like we intended it too, we can go in and fix that specific bill without having to redo the entire big bill. I feel that is how we must tackle this problem since I get what Nancy Pelosi is saying. Then we don't have to keep writing on them and voting on them cause what we do is write them all on its own paper and bring them to the floor and vote on each one separately that we agree on. Then the one's we don't, we find out if this is what *We the People* want. We look into the overall safety of the issue and if it's correct, we go back to the floor and we tell them who's holding our vote up. That way in the 2018 mid-term election *We the People* know who to get rid of. This is how every bill in our government should be done. Every time you want to throw in the entire kitchen sink, even though it's done with great intentions, most times it just doesn't work that way. They say when you have a lot of People making decisions "too many cooks spoil the broth" or "too many Chiefs and not enough Indians." That's what we got to do, a check list on all of our common-sense gun laws (please see my list at the end) and enact them all like we've enacted our own safety driving laws. You must get a license, you must register your car. With driving we have auto insurance, so with firearms do we require a person to have insurance? I mean there are a lot of questions that we can ask and need answers too. The key is to proceed effectively on this issue cause if one thinks that we just walk in there and ban assault weapons, modify a few laws and – Wahlah! – our gun problem here in America is fixed, then I'm sorry to say we are fooling ourselves. Then to fix one problem without fixing the ton of others is again fooling ourselves. What they say, "setting ourselves up for failure" or "trying to put a band aid on a gunshot wound". It simply won't work! If we do that we would not only be fooling ourselves, but we would be living in Trumps 'White House of an altered universe', it's just not realistic. What we need is a realistic common-sense gun plan to slow the problem cause the only way to ever stop the entire problem is to take all the guns, which won't happen. However, common-sense does say that we need to get to the root of our problem, which the common denominator of the problem is the guns. Like they say, "you weed whack the weeds and they will grow back tomorrow, but if you go out and pull the weeds, those weeds won't grow back.

To tackle our gun issue, we can look at it as having a massive garden that we mis-managed and allowed it to get over grown. We look at it and don't know where to start. We see common-sense things that need to be done like trimming back the hedges. Nancy Pelosi's analogy of the "grass needs to be mowed here and there" and we all can agree on these things, but we're back to it's so overwhelming that we don't know where to start. Honestly, I just faced this same issue in writing this book. This latest massacre (and I'm sure that by the time this book goes to print it will be the second latest massacre or even the third) and our overall gun violence problem here in America is so overwhelming that I really didn't know where to start. What do I say? To be honest I'm still at that point right now with half of this book written, but I realized about a third of the way through is just to say what needs to be said. So, I say, that is what we just need to do – what needs to be done. Just like this book, when I'm done I hope I said everything I wanted to say.

That's why I say bear with me cause my grammar might not be there and hey I really don't care. To me I would only think that if someone was worried about my grammar of how I said it, then they obviously missed the message. So please judge me on my content and not my grammar. For real, I'm sitting here with a stack of notes, flipping from page to page, trying to find the right words to say, and when I'm done I hope that I did. That's all I can ask for in the end, other than, NEVER AGAIN! Other than that, I'm trying, and we are going to fake it till we make it, so please bear with me as I try to put it all in the right context at the right time.

However, to get back to my point before I get lost talking about myself, we got to come up with a plan of what we want and how we want it, then we demand action on it. In reality our checklist for gun safety is going to be long. We are not all instantly going to agree on all of them, but if we tackle each one we agree on first and then fire whomever doesn't agree with us and get the rest. That's why doing everything one by one separately will work. That way we get immediate action on what we agree on and we know exactly who to fire come the next election cycle: *People who do not have our (and our kids) best interest at heart.* It's a way of weeding out the People that are for us and the People that are against us, "We had a reasonable demand" and he said "...B.S.", well then, he got to go, period. Sorry about his luck, but we must put our safety and security above him having a job. My only hope would be that he doesn't spit in our food when we go to McDonald's and buy a happy meal, cause leave it to me he definitely would be starting off at a low-level position again. At this point, we are better off employing a High Schooler to Congress than a numbskull that's committing treason for going against 70% of the American People for no apparent reason.

That's why I'm proposing a one bill, one vote system. That way nothing is intricate, and nothing gets overwhelming or intoxicating. It's like what I'm doing with this book, sure I want to skip to the end, but if I don't keep writing from right here I'm never going to make it to the end. To be honest, I don't even know what the end is going to say other than MARCH FOR OUR LIVES! Then probably, THE END....OMG! That's all 1 know I don't even know what I'm going to say next, I'm just making it up as I go along, for real. I guess that's the beauty of this being my book, I can say what I want and think. Thank God we do have a First Amendment Right to 'free speech' cause some of the stuff I've said already... I might be in trouble for in another country. But that's why I'm American and live in America so I can be free to say and do as I please, as long as it's not against the law and I am in trouble with the law, and/or better yet, they're in trouble with me, but that is another story for another time. At this point I would just like to say, 'Hi' and I hope you're having a great day or at least the best it can be. However, if we want to stick around and see tomorrow, we must tackle our gun violence issues TODAY. As of right now, we're in for a world of trouble if we don't. There is just going to be more school shootings, and more shootings, and more killings period. That's why I say, if we can't stop the gun violence here in our own backyard, then we won't never be able to stop it abroad. I think the saying is, "if we can't get the plank out of our own eyes, then we won't be able to get the plank out of anyone else's". I'll tell you what, gun violence here in America is really a plank in our eye that we absolutely must get rid of.

Then once we come up with a solution to stop gun violence here at home, then and only then... can we solve the gun violence issue abroad. We have had two wars going on forever that has just been a sword in our side cause this is a lot bigger than just a thorn. The Afghanistan war is our longest running war in United States History. 17 years and counting... We have spent over 6000 days there, spent over 50 Billion each year there and the Taliban is still in control. They have more guns and drugs than ever before and ISIS as everyone knows is out of control. What are we doing? I feel our President and Congress don't know how to end the war because they have no clue of what to do. We see that on our own gun issue problem. They don't even want to implement common-sense gun laws here at home, so I dare not ask what they are doing abroad. But I know whatever it is, it's not working! To be honest, they don't even know how to stop the fighting amongst themselves, let alone stop the fighting of our foreign and/or domestic terrorists. The fighting in our House Intel Committee has gotten so freaking bad between the Democrats and the Republicans that they are going to build a wall in between themselves cause they don't trust each other. But I'll tell you what, if they don't trust each other... then how are we to trust any of them? Then what? When one side has valuable information they're not going to pass it onto the other side, so we can do something about it. I mean honestly is this how the FBI information wasn't passed on about Nikolas Cruz from the Washington, D.C., field office to the Miami field office cause some kind of internal dispute that they're not telling us about or something?

I mean there are so many questions *We the People* must consider, and so many variables we must take into account in order to get to the root cause of our problem, especially since this is an all-American issue. The problem is really... *What are we going to do about it?* For some reason... the Republicans love to deregulate everything. I honestly believe the root of that reasoning is money. That's why our economy is appearing to do so well, cause they deregulated everything, but at what expense to our Country is the Question. The Stock Market has ballooned to an all-time high, but we are in another financial bubble which will – *POP* – and come crashing down on us like it did in 2008. They want to do more off-shore drilling for oil. For what? So, we can have another catastrophe gulf-oil spill.

It's like, if we take off the speed limit and governors on cars, are we going to have more accidents. Well, history has proven – *yes*... it does. A higher speed limit does significantly increase the danger to public safety on our roads. Now we turn that analogy back to gun violence and question whether or not the sale of commercial assault rifles in America significantly increases the danger of public safety. And, again, history has proven – *yes*... it does. Just the sale alone, of larger magazine clips increases the danger of public safety, so if we can answer "*yes*... it does" on that – then surely the sale of these high-powered combat assault-style war weapons does too. It's that simple! Since the lifting of the ban in 2004 by George W. Bush, and the Republican party, mass shootings with this style of weaponry has increased by 200%.

At 51%, I would say that these combat assault rifles more likely than not, significantly increase the danger to our public safety. I mean, even when we look at our legal standard of attorney incompetence, under well-known U.S. Supreme Court precedent in: Strickland v. Washington, 466 U.S. 668 (1984), you'll find that attorney incompetence is deemed at something less than 50%. So, to make my point, where we are talking about an increase of gun violence by 200% with the sale of these weapons. We seriously have to be freaking nuts, as a Nation, to keep selling them. 51% is asking for trouble, 200% is begging for it. 200% is what we see manifested in our Nation TODAY. Our kids are dying left and right cause of it and when it comes to our kids dying, it's not a left or right issue. *It's all of OUR issue.*

Just think if we increased the current speed limit from 55-65-70 miles-per-hour up to 200 miles-per-hour. Then sold everyone a car or truck that went fast, we'll have a 200% or more increase in wrecks and fatalities on our roads. That's what we're seeing here with these guns. By allowing these war-style assault weapons, with clips that are extended, and bump stocks (fully automatic accessories), to be sold in a commercial fashion. Our streets have already witnessed the most massive shooting in modern day history, with the Las Vegas Massacre. But that's only if we look at this issue in isolation! If we seriously sit down and remove our tunnel vision on this issue, from a broadband spectrum position, we can see the whole picture and the opening of our eyes this wide is… (I don't even have the word for it cause the totality of these massacres are that indescribable)

The crazy part is there is no end in sight, unless we stand together and start doing something about it TODAY. I mean our President and Republican Leaders can sit on their hands all they want too, which they have done for years on this issue. I'm sorry to say it again, but I'm going to say it again and again and again and … Maybe that's why they were all on board that train accident the morning after Trumps 2018 State of the Union Address speech; so maybe they'd wake up and smell the coffee. I mean I hate to say it like that, but there is no other way to say it! Then What? All Republicans do is go back to pointing the finger about abortions. I watched this same issue unfold on FOX NEWS the other day and it tends to happen a lot. Trump is the grandmaster wizard at it. Every time someone asks him what he is going to do about it, he instantly goes into what Obama, or past administrations did, or shouldn't have done.

Well, my whole thing is… if Trump and the Republicans can sit up there and ask why Obama and the Democrats didn't tackle gun legislation when they controlled the White House and Congress… *Right then and there they are acknowledging that we have a problem…* but then THEY don't want to fix the problem. *Why?* Because they're freaking getting paid not to! So, my question to you is, *"If We the People know about it – then what are We the People going to do about it?"*, cause it's obvious that our elected officials are being paid off and this is the root of all of our problems. We fix that, and we are more likely than not to fix the entire system. Yes, we tackle gun violence TODAY, but we still have an opioid problem tomorrow. We look at that issue and again many of our elected officials have been bought off by pharmaceutical companies that have been Lobbying (or better yet, colluding with our public officials and meddling in our elections for years). The whirlwind has gotten so bad on the do-nothing federal level, that now you see individual states, like Kentucky (the 5th highest rate of opioid overdoses in the Country) recently propose a 25% Tariff on every opioid dose the drug companies distribute to the state, cause they're sending an average of 417 pills for every person in like, 5 counties. I'll tell you what, the numbers are astronomical (something way out), so when we hear Trump and our politicians stand up there and state they're doing all they can to end the opioid epidemic in our Country, *it's all a bunch of baloney*. History is still showing us why this is, and *We the People* must do something about it.

Of course, not to get off topic cause we are talking about gun violence here in America, but we must not turn a blind eye to the known fact that our President and politicians are being bought off not to act as we speak. That's why we can't get nothing we need done. And that's like what Thomas Jefferson said once, *"We the people* are the only sure reliance for the preservation of our liberty." William Hazlitt once said, "There is not a more mean, stupid, dastardly, pitiful, selfish, spiteful, envious, ungrateful animal than the public. It is the greatest of cowards, for it is afraid of itself." That statement in and of itself makes sense to me cause the NRA is made up of nothing more than ourselves. Deep down inside everyone that's got rational thinking, has a pretty common opinion, but then we kind of don't want to act cause it hasn't really hit close enough to home, so to speak. But look, our kids are dying here at home, so… wake up! It has hit America, OUR HOME!

It's kind of like the kids said, "if this happened to them and their kids then they would be more on board to do something about it." But, I along with these kids are telling you, the time to act is now. Please don't wait to try to act when it gets closer to "your home" (or yet hits "your home"). Cause then it will be all too late. You see, I haven't said much about that school officer, Scot Peterson, which to me there is no other reason than his cowardice for his failure to act in this particular situation, especially since I'm pretty sure he received a lot of training on how to respond to an active shooter over his 30 years of being a deputy. Therefore, simply put, no excuse! I'm just using this as an example right here in order to show you the magnitude of this type of assault rifle, a weapon of war. Again, there is no excuses cause he should have engaged that shooter. I'm just showing you a prime example of how the rapid fire of this particular weapon can stop a 30-year veteran officer dead in his tracks, with terror, from acting. Even when he must have heard the cries of kids dying. Even when he had training for 30 years, I can say nothing other than the sounds of the semi-automatic shots were freaking frightening to him. And I'm saying this because that's why we have to get these assault weapons off of our streets. (Yeah, he was a coward cause the sounds of that assault rifle are scary).

Now Trump can sit up there… and say whatever in the heck he wants to about running in this school with no gun, cause it's only a few people would… I know that, and I can tell you from instinct… Trump can talk that crap… but he doesn't have one characteristic of a hero! More like a zero!!! Trump is just not one of those you can see being a hero. He won't even stand up to his base or the NRA right now and he's already the Freaking President. So... what makes you think he would stand up to a hail of gunfire, when he can't even stand up to these people who's not even holding an imaginary weapon.

Then like they said from day one... Trumps a draft dodger to begin with! Stand up, yeah right! What they say, Trumps all talk... like a chihuahua – all bark and no bite, just another prime example of how his statement of running into the school was just another bad joke, at a time when nothing about this is freaking funny. If anything, he's the freaking joke and that's why he keeps flip-flopping on this freaking issue or playing around. Like he's a kid in a daycare center or a freaking playground. What they say, he's flirting with the ideas. I keep telling myself that I'm going to write this out as it comes out and I'm sorry cause what's coming to my mind at this time is if he wanted to flirt with an idea, he should have flirted with those women, instead he sexually assaulted and harassed them. That was the time to flirt. Now, when it's time to assault and harass these guns laws or lack thereof, he wants to flirt with ideas. To me it just fits right into his character, to assault and harass the innocent, but when it comes to standing up to the NRA and his base he can't do it. What a real bum. Tell him I said he needs to go pull the tape of the Las Vegas Concert shooting and take a good, hard, long look at it. Cause if he was in that crowd, he sure wouldn't have been running toward that shooter holding a machine gun. Even if he had a gun, he probably wouldn't even have pulled it out and fired it in the direction of the shooter. To be honest... I could say more, but *why*... but then...

Or else, tell him this... since he was brave enough to do something there, then be brave enough to do something now (see, that's what I thought) and it's not even about calling his bluff. I've always been a man about action and he doesn't appear to have one ounce of it. Honor and integrity (Yeah... He doesn't have it!). Sorry, but more Like... lies and deceit. He claims he would have ran in and saved those kids, but he's so scary that he won't even run his office and sign a Bill that could potentially save the lives of more kids. Yeah, right... What's the saying: "I was born at night, but not last night." It's like that other saying from, Henry Ward Beecher: "When men sell eleven ounces for twelve, he makes a compact with the devil, and sells himself for the value of an ounce."

To me, that's what they are all doing. They sold their souls to the devil for an ounce, when those kids lives, those people's lives, and our own lives, are priceless. I'm sorry, that's why all those top Republicans had that train accident (ALL ABOARD)! "They thought they hit a cow, cause in their minds they probably thought, Holy Cow! But they found out they hit a dump truck, just like we found out they're a bunch of dump trucks!

OMG, I'm so sorry, I just get so mad at how they've been representing us and how everything's been going. How these kids can cry out for help and these people still refuse to help them, only because their own agenda is to help themselves to as much pocket change as they can... scoundrels. I bet you that's why a lot of Republicans are leaving Congress cause they don't want to be a part of this madness and corruption anymore. And I mean, I can keep talking about this until I'm blue in the face and my hands fall off from writing it. However, to make a long story short we seriously have to implement a new ban on these assault weapons and drastically change gun laws now. Until we get to that point, let's...

MARCH FOR OUR LIVES!!!

MARCH FOR OUR LIVES!!!

If anyone takes MONEY from the NRA
during the 2018 Campaign,
THEIR Campaign will be D.O.A.!!!

Chris Hixon

D O A... "Dead On Arrival", cause if killing their campaign is what it takes to get comprehensive gun reforms to pass, then so be it. I'd rather see their campaign hopes be D.O.A. then the next kid from a massive gun shooting. That's why I say... if they take money from the NRA – we got to make sure their campaign is D.O.A. The same if they take money from the Pharmaceutical Companies – we have to make their campaign D.O.A.

We really need to be voting for the candidate who spends the less money on their campaign cause at that point we can assume he has the less people in his pocket. Like Senator Marco Rubio said, "he's not going to stop taking money from the NRA" and you know what – his 2018 campaign should be D.O.A. I mean a lot of people wanted to give him credit for showing up at the CNN Town Hall Meeting, in wake of this MSDHS shooting. But to me… that was his job since he specifically represents the state of Florida. He had to show up cause those were his constituents. Now maybe I would give him an ounce of credit for changing his position on large-capacity round magazines, but nowhere close to the ton of credit some people wanted to give him. Especially since after that meeting he was nowhere close to the freaking TON of guns laws we must implement in our Nation in order to keep our kids, our schools, our communities and all of us safe.

Now if Rubio was say representing Utah or something like that and he showed up to talk to these kids from Florida then I would give him a few more ounces of credit and a ton of courage for taking on these kid's tough questions, but Sen. Marco Rubio's 2018 Campaign – at the end of the day in my opinion, should be D.O.A. He sat in front of these kids and parents and quite frankly gave us his opinion on gun reform that more or less sucked. He was simply pathetically weak on this issue just like our President. Yeah... he showed up when Trump didn't. But the facts remain the same, especially since everyone knows that Trump is weak minded all ready. If it wasn't for his father teaching him real estate and funding his earlier projects, he never would have made it. Even if his story of his father only giving him 1 Million Dollars is true, 1 Million Dollars in the early 70's is definitely over 10 Million Dollars TODAY. So… to Trump… "Save it please!" Anyhow, where was I… cause I just got caught up in wanting to constantly berate Trump's behavior and it's not even cause I'm a Donald Trump hater, but it's cause Donald Trump thinks that everything is a game and to me he is the most freaking, worst, most inconsistent, unfair player.

I just don't know sometimes! All I can say is heartless, cause even if he (Trump) wasn't going to show up to the CNN Town Hall Meeting for whatever reason (he simply doesn't like CNN) he should have – at least to me – sent a White House representative down there to answer those kids and their parent's questions. I know what they always say, "but were talking about Donald Trump here...". Yeah, I know and that just goes to the point I'm trying to make is that his lack of real empathy and understanding as a leader sucks, for real. Every time you see it, it just shocks the conscious of how cold-blooded these people can be. I mean, yeah, we knew he was a snake before we took him in, but a lot of people thought he was like a Gardener or something? This dude is like a real Anaconda trying to eat people. To tell the truth I've been waiting on Ice Cube and TV Crew to come in and save me and you. Tell the movie director cut, cause this new Anaconda Trump movie sucks. Or better yet, Trump was the guy that was trying to get us all ate by the Anaconda cause I can see now that's how this plot is going.

And I'm sorry to tell you but we better be doing something now before we be the next plot, Or worse yet, be in Trump's next State of the Union speech about a kid putting a flag on our plot. No offense, but I'm serious cause if you think we are going to get by in this world without no real major gun reform, then I'm telling you right now... We are really up shit creek without a paddle. just waiting on the next gunman to pull the fire alarm that will herd our kids to him, so he can slaughter them like cattle. So, whoever you are... and whatever your name is... I'm here to tell you that the March For Our Lives issue is clearly not a game. Here we are really Marching for OUR LIVES.

That's why I tell you that if any of our politicians take money from the NRA – we must make their campaign D.O.A. I mean did you see that lady spokeswoman from the NRA, Dana Loesch, during the CNN Town Hall Meeting, her non-verbal communication toward the kids was sour. She had an attitude from the very beginning. Her answers were cold-blooded and cruel. She appeared to have no empathy, sympathy, compassion, nor understanding for these kids, their parents, their plight or ours. Nothing she said was even in a kind manner. That's why it came as no surprise when she said "The media loves mass shootings... they love the ratings" I'm thinking, how crazy can this lady be? No wonder why she's the spokeswoman for the NRA, she definitely was a piece of work and a cold-blooded, unhappy, four-legged, female dog (that's for sure)!

Man, I'm sorry, but I got to say that like it is. I try to sugar coat it as much as I can, but wow, her words and posture was way out. As soon as she opened her mouth I was hoping they were just going to 'escort' her out the building, "like Ma'am (or little doggy), we don't have nothing to say to you!" For real as soon as she got up to leave the whole audience should have said, "Bye Felisha!" Y'all think I'm playing! Where do they find these kinds of people at! Especially to a woman with kids… in the face of crying kids and crying parents and she acted like that. If I was her husband I would want a divorce or better yet, I would never have married her in the first place. Yeah, I would have gave her a promise alright, a promise to never show up around her ever again. What they say… MARCH FOR OUR LIVES!... I'm sorry, but she had no sorrow and to be honest I have no sorrow in berating her. Hopefully she hears about it. She'll find out when her husband runs for the hills, she'll ask him, "Where are you going?" He'll respond "I'm going for a run… I'll be back", as he turns around and says under his breath MARCH FOR OUR LIVES!

You know what? Never in my weirdest dreams have I seen so many of our elected officials unempathetic when it comes to a major catastrophe like the MSDHS shooting. I see now why we didn't get no gun legislation passed through Congress in wake of the Sandy Hook Elementary School shooting. They just have no empathy whatsoever. To be honest I'm not a Democrat or Republican, but if I was a Republican with the morals that they have shown under this Republican party's, sorry excuse of a leadership... I would jump off the bandwagon TODAY. Anyone that doesn't care about fixing a broken system that allows criminals to get weapons of war and shoot kids is not a party I want to be affiliated with. And, they can look at the MSDHS shooting all they want and say this guy legally purchased this firearm, nor was he a criminal. They can act dumb all they want too but they know that cause of these gun show loopholes, guns show up on our streets in places like Chicago and are used to gun down innocent people every day. So, I don't want to hear the load of crap or pitch of fried ice cream they're trying to sell themselves or us. What they need to do is tell themselves the truth and get on the right side of history before the next raving lunatic with a gun shoots them and they be the ones that's history.

One thing I can tell you for sure and this is to combat what Sen. Marco Rubio said at the CNN Town Hall Meeting and that was something to the effect of "he doesn't buy into the agenda of the NRA... they buy into his." And you know what I'm going to tell you is... B.S.! All that was, was a great line of crap! The NRA or any Company is not going to give someone endorsements that don't fully endorse their agenda. Sprite is not going to pay me to do a commercial to drink Coke. Ford is not going to pay me to do a commercial when I drive a Chevrolet. It's like water and oil, it don't mix; it never has, and it never will. No matter how many times you shake it or slosh it around or put it in a blender, in the end it will still separate the same. So... he can try to separate himself from them as much as he wants to. But, he's definitely aligned with the NRA's agendas or else they wouldn't endorse him, especially with no 3.3

Million Dollars. He received more money from the NRA (3.3 Million Dollars), as a Congressman, than the President would make in two terms (8 years of being President). The presidency only makes $400,000 a year, times 8 years is only 3.2 Million Dollars, so believe me when I tell you he got paid to look the other way. Then when you look at Trump… he's gotten 31 Million Dollars from the NRA which is 10 times more than he would have received as President for 8 years and to think he's only been in there a little more than a year. Yet he already got 10 times more than if he was President for the entire 8! Yeah… these people are paid off and if we want something done we got to either pay them off or cast them off. (Let's just vote them off the island.)

The craziest part is they are getting paid from both sides. In one hand, we're paying them money to work for us, and in the other hand they're collecting money to work against us. I mean how do we even compete. We're actually in a Trade War, where they are getting paid 10 times more as a matter of fact, cause they take our money and still not doing nothing. Trump's always talking about how Russia is laughing at us, but I bet you he's the one that's really laughing at us and that's where he got it from.

Then the people who support these leaders of the Republican party can think they're in on the fray and laughing with them. But I keep telling you none of these mass shooters have cared whether the people he was shooting at was Democrat or Republican. The maniac in Las Vegas didn't give a rat's ass who he was shooting at. The guy who shot up the church in Texas didn't care who he was shooting at either. None of them did! Don't think for one second, they even thought to stop and ask if this was a Democratic church or a Republican concert. They didn't care. That's why I say, "this is not a Democratic or a Republican issue… *This is an American issue*". To be honest, if the leaders of the Republican party didn't want to change the laws after Sandy Hook and now after this Marjory Stoneman Douglas High School shooting, that if I was a member of this Republican party, I would dump them like a bad habit rabbit.

The Republicans are sitting back, knowing they can possibly prevent another mass shooting from occurring and they do nothing... for the love of money... so believe me that is no one I want to be associated with. They can potentially save lives and don't want too. *For real!* Let's be honest, they can pass legislation that more likely than not would save future lives and they don't want too. They would rather allow it to happen, they would rather do nothing. In my mind that's like being an accessory to murder. We could have prevented our kids from being killed in the future, yet we stood still and allowed it to happen. I swear, that's no different than being an accomplice, to me. That's like what the NRA spokeswomen Dana Doggy said, "the media loves mass shootings; they love the ratings", or worse yet standing on the outside of the door like Scot Peterson did, and don't run in to stop the shooter. Cowards I tell you. Bought off Cowards.

Cause it must be them (the NRA) that loves these mass shootings. That's why she got up there in the CNN Town Hall Meeting, with such a funky attitude, cause she can't figure out why everybody doesn't love these mass shootings, like her. I mean most everyone in that building had a sympathetic look on their faces – but her – and I'm sorry... but I can't get over that. Go rewind the tape and take a look around... then hear her hateful words "the media loves it". Yeah, that lady is crazy! Cuckoo for serial killers!!! (weirdo)!!!

You know what, this is the last thing I'm going to tell you before I close this Chapter, cause I get frustrated really fast knowing that people are really dying, and our elected officials are doing nothing about it. Believe me if our government knows that our gun background check is wholly unvetted and has been forever… if our government is knowing that the gun show Loophole allows people every day, people like dangerous criminals and other domestic terrorists, to get their hands on guns, that's really killing people every day (all those shootings you don't see on TV) and it's been going on forever… and if our government, by at least a preponderance of evidence, has gotten paid by the NRA to do nothing about it… *please tell me* how our government is not aiding and abetting these maniac's in these murders?

The fact that our government has known that these criminals have gotten their hands on these guns through an unvetted background check and/or gun show loophole forever; and that these guns have been used on our streets to kill people forever; plus coupled with the fact that our government officials have been paid off to do not a thing, is treasonous to the American People. Like I say, the people of the Republican party can look the other way, but I will tell you one thing for sure, two things for certain, and that is 1) Those bullets don't have a party affiliation to them, and 2) That means they are also committing treasonous acts against themselves too.

So please don't say you haven't been warned. I know it sounds like we're crying wolf, we're crying wolf, we're crying wolf; but you got to remember, that in this analogy you're still a sheep. Even if the Republican party leaders are not the direct wolves, they have been getting paid to leave the gun show loophole gate wide open. (The survey says a minimum of 40% open). This, so the wolves can come in and eat us. We are paying them to keep us safe and guard the gate, and they are getting paid 10 times the amount to leave the gate open. *THAT'S TREASON*. I'm not lying! Let's look up the definition. Here we go… Treason: "The betrayal of one's Country, esp. by aiding an enemy."

I mean can somebody please tell me how our government is not aiding the enemy (criminals, gangs, Bloods and Crips, MS-13, the KKK) to get real weapons of war by *their refusal* to implement universal background checks and close gun show loopholes on the sale of firearms, not to mention the ability to get guns on Craig's List, which has gone on (FOREVER) here in America? For real, this means that they have been betraying us, *We the People* of the United States, by aiding the enemy to get guns to kill us with here in America (FOREVER). Man, if that's not treason, I don't know what is! And, if the People of the Republican party in this Country don't want to believe that then they are just blind to the facts. One thing I do know is that I believe it isn't that they can't see the solution… it's that they can't really see the problem. To them it's not a big deal, but politicians are the ones getting paid the big deal. All while *We the People* are getting a treasonous deal. And, you can keep turning a blind eye to these treasonous acts of our government if you want to. AND it's not just been with guns – it has been with this opioid epidemic that's been killing a lot of people as well. So again, they turn a blind eye to this message if they want too. I'll tell you one last thing for sure, if the blind leads the blind, both shall fall into a ditch. So… you can turn a blind eye, or you can stand up with us till we win, cause our goal is not to lose our kids, me, or you, behind their treasonous actions… Everybody stand up and say…

MARCH FOR OUR LIVES!!!

MARCH FOR OUR LIVES!!!

CHAPTER 8

Our Nation is Heartbroken
AND WE THE PEOPLE want Action...

Luke Hoyer

I don't know about you, but I have been heartbroken ever since I heard the news of yet another school shooting. It has literally been heart-wrenching to see these kids cry. It made me only think of my own daughters who are now in high school. My baby girl is 14 years old and in the 9th grade. An amazing kid and straight 'A' student, just like her dad. I guess knowing that, I'm sorry... I can't even find the words of what I feel or what I should say, except for *heartbreaking*, especially when I couple that with the knowledge of what I said at the close of last Chapter and then my heartbreak turns to anger.

It was like watching that dad at the CNN Town Hall Meeting, who bravely got up there to ask a question after losing his daughter. I'm going to be honest cause after he-said he lost his daughter in this horrific shooting, I didn't hear the question he asked after that, nor did I hear the answer. As I'm processing it right now my mind draws a blank as to what was said. Maybe it did so in order to protect me from ever having to witness such an up-front, close, and personal horrific story and/or I was just too angry to hear anything after that. I could still see the dad's face, the pain, the hurt, the suffering, but looking back on it, I can't remember what he said. I mean he stood there for a long time too. Then came the answer; but I didn't hear the answer either and maybe cause there is no answer that would ever make me feel better. I can ask a question all day long as to *why?* our government didn't do anything after the first school shooting (way back when) and/or *why?* wasn't the first school shooting, the last school shooting? To me there is no question I could ever have asked or an answer I would care to hear, unless he looked me dead in the eyes and told me the truth **'Its cause they simply don't care!'**

That's the only answer I could have went for, the truth! Because in so many words that's what they've been telling us and telling us again and again by refusing to fix the problem is: "WE DON'T CARE." The crazy part is it's not even like their failing to act out of ignorance or incompetence (that would be one thing), but they have literally, flat out, refused to act after Sandy Hooks' massacre in 2012; the recent church massacre, the Pulse Nightclub shooting, the Las Vegas Concert shooting. The list just goes on and on and on, to the Chicago, L.A., and New York shootings you don't really hear about. But they know, and then on and on again to now, where we are at the 18th School Shooting of just 2018 alone. (didn't really hear nothing or too much about the past 17 shootings of 2018) Then we get three weeks after the MSDHS massacre, where 17 more kids and teachers have died – 15 more seriously wounded, that thank God, they're alive, and Donald Trump and the Republican Leaders have again refused to implement anything more before this. Anything???… well certainly not Common-Sense Gun Laws. (*ARE YOU FREAKING KIDDING ME???*)

And, like I said, these bullets don't freaking have a party affiliation, they don't care whether you're Republican or Democrat, male or female, kid or adult, so what this entire administration is telling all of us, *We the people*, is simply… "THEY DON'T CARE! … THEY DON'T CARE! … THEY DON'T CARE!!!" I mean what else can we think but "THEY DON'T CARE?" Especially since they haven't done nothing since the previous shootings. *We the People*, the American people, are getting sold-out by our government and *We the People* must demand action.

As matter of fact, *We the People* are demanding action now! They think we are playing with them cause honestly, we have been. We have been letting them slide and get away with doing nothing for so long, for far, far, too long. I honestly feel that they think this is going to go away like it has in the past, but you know what… not TODAY! Not this time, we are not going away!!! They are not going to be able to just sweep this under the rug especially, when they done it for far too long. It's time that they either start working for us, or we get some new people in there that will. It's that simple. We give them our demands and we demand action.

Like I say… don't get me started cause if it was left up to me I'm demanding that they… fix everything (EVERY FREAKING THING) in 90 days, or else they can go ahead and deregulate everything for the next 5 months after that cause come November 2018 mid-term election *It's Over*. I would burn grass with them.

And, trust and believe me, they're old enough to know what that means. Cause this is flat out ridiculous. There is no possible way we should be sitting here putting up with half of this crap TODAY. Like Martin Luther King Jr. said once,

"Injustice anywhere is a threat to justice everywhere!" and I'll tell you what… government officials are getting paid off to turn a blind eye here, then they're getting paid to turn a blind eye everywhere. There is no difference and in any case, injustice is being heaped upon us, the American People, any way we look at it. They have the NRA – that's only 5 million people – buying off our public officials who are making decisions for all 325 Million of us. The fraction of the NRA is so small compared to the total amount of American People here in the U.S., that it's almost incomputable, to what, 65%. Therefore, there is no way that we should allow 5 million people to control what 70% of us 325 Million people want done. It's just that simple...

I mean, what, like 70% of 325 million is about 227.5 Million People. So, 227.5 Million people are on record saying we want stricter gun laws here in America and we are going to allow 5 Million people to stand in our way of achieving it. Somewhere along the line the other 25-30 % of America wants something done on gun legislation as well. To be honest, the 25-30% remaining just might be the younger kids cause every adult I know wants stricter gun legislation and they want it sooner rather than later. So, our American Government can keep playing if they want too, but there is no way that we are going to allow the 5 million people in the NRA control what we… 227.5 Million of the American people… want done here TODAY. They can keep paying our President and the people in Congress if they want to. But… come November we must put our foot down and either we get what we want. or we vote them all out and still get what we want. Our government makes it seem like it's so hard to get legislation through Congress, but all they have to do is draft a Bill and sign it. There's nothing complicated about that. Like, Winston Churchill stated, *We the People* demand "Victory at all cost, victory in spite of all terror, victory however long and hard the road may be; for without victory there is no survival", for you or for me.

And that victory has to come with a victory on gun legislation cause without victory on gun legislation, someone, somewhere, here in America is not going to survive until old-age. That's just a fact. If school shootings are more common than winning the lottery right now, then we might not even have until next month to act (and we didn't) and that's just a hard fact. Lives are on the line every day and the more time we waste waiting on what Trump and Congress is going to do, we are going to lose a few dozen more.

I say forget what they are doing or what they are thinking about doing. *We the People* – all 227.5 Million of us – that are demanding action need to put on paper our demands and put Trump and Congress on notice that the failure to meet our demands during the time frame we are demanding it will result in their rejection in our next election. Like Vincent Lombardi had said: "Winning isn't everything, it's the only thing"! That's why I say, we are not walking away from this issue a loser. If anyone's going to lose, it's going to be them losing cause their seat in the next election is not guaranteed. Cause we are going to win no matter what. If it's the Super Bowl and we need to play, then we are going to pull out the "Philly Special" TODAY. They know what that is!

It's like what Knute Rockne said. "Show me a good and gracious loser and I'll show you a failure." We're – not – going to go away till 'we win'. There is no good or gracious loser and we the American people aren't going to start by being one TODAY. Especially since we are losing our kid's lives, and our own lives.

That's why I say, "it's not a game" and yes, I do have poor sportsmanship when it comes to this issue, cause I play for the American team and there is no way I'm going to stand on the sidelines and let 5 million people of the NRA beat us 227.5 Million people TODAY. It just don't work that way.

Then what do we have… less than 550-600 people in our Presidency and Congress. 100 in the Senate and like, 400 something in the House, so less than 600 people. How in the heck are we going to let less than 600 people tell us 227.5 Million people what they are or are not going to do? These people got to be gone crazy and we are gone insane if we allow it to happen any longer.

This is outrageous! We have allowed the Lobbyist Corporations to buy-off the 600 people that make the decisions for us. That's why we see people like Donald Trump, our very own President, getting paid 31 Million Dollars from the NRA… or Senator Marco Rubio getting paid 3.3 million dollars from the NRA… to sell us out TODAY. Trust and believe more are getting paid a lot more as well. The crazy part is they don't even have to buy-off all 600 of them, cause all they have to do is buy-off half… Two-thirds and they got us for sure. We let them buy-off two-thirds of Congress (less than 400 people) to not do what over two-thirds of the entire American People want done. So, we allow 400 people to tell us 227.5 Million people what to do? Yeah right… maybe yesterday… but not TODAY, not tonight, and definitely not tomorrow!

How do 227.5 Million people tell 400 people what to do and they tell us "NO" – they are not going to change gun laws. 400 people tell us "THEY DON'T CARE". We act like we don't care by allowing them to get away with it. I'm serious… cause we are allowing 400 people which in reality is probably less than 300 people on this issue, tell us – 200-300 Million people – *what they*

Aren't going to do. To tell you the truth I feel irate right now. We should have been got rid of these people by now.

We have allowed pretty much these same 600 people, give or take a few, to drag us into 2 wars, and spend at least 15 TRILLION Dollars on our credit card, since Bush Jr. era, and do a whole host of everything else while they get paid to play. I mean we just had our stupid President playing golf on President's Day, when people are laying their kids to rest that day. Funerals were held nearby and he's out playing golf, smiling! Yeah, I heard the heck out of that one. I mean, if we don't stand up and demand action right now, then *We the People* aren't going to get action right now.

We have allowed these 600 people to control what we're doing here in America and they're all bought-off in some scope or fashion. They have someone in their pocket and someone in they're ear. If we don't boot these people out on their butts as soon as possible, we got to be nuts. And, I may be a little crazy now, cause we have sat back and put up with this craziness far too long. We have allowed these 600 people to commit treason against us 325 million people. No wonder why I feel like I'm getting a bald spot on my head… cause I keep scratching my head wondering how we are continuously allowing this to happen.

I guess it's like Napoleon Bonaparte said, "If you want a thing done well… do it yourself." So… if we the American people – *which is over 227.5 Million of us* – want stricter gun legislation, and really want this to happen, we got to do it ourselves. We got to come up with exactly what we want and make them do exactly what we want. It's like watching the CNN Town Hall Meeting, where mostly everyone in the room was from Florida. Thousands of People that want to ban assault rifles and get stricter gun laws and we sat there and watched Senator Marco Rubio – *one person* – sit there and tell us what he's willing to support, or not. Especially, after he sat there and admitted that he has taken millions of dollars from the NRA and he's willing to accept millions more if they offer it.

Yeah right, I heard that one, heard it all now! I still can't even believe it. It's unbelievable, how I sat there and watched 5-10 Thousand People tell – one person – what they wanted and Senator Marco Rubio, just pretty much said "NO"! Man... how pathetic is that? I was literally appalled and rendered speechless! For crying out loud, we must get our heads out of the sand and demand action, cause you know what... We got too...

MARCH FOR OUR LIVES!!!

See SOMETHING, Say SOMETHING!

-FBI

Cara Loughran

You know what? The FBI has always said "If you see something, say something", but I'm here to tell them "If you hear something, do something!" Because the People of Parkland, Florida saw something and said something, and the FBI admitted to hearing something, *yet – they did nothing!*

They literally had several phone calls from people asserting that Nikolas Cruz was planning, potentially, to conduct a school shooting and no one did nothing about it. I mean, *WOW!* ... if we are only as strong as our weakest link then *We the People* must find out where the chain was broken and fix it. If we think that we are only looking at one or two weak links in our chain, we really need to stop thinking cause thinking is not our best asset. We really have to sit down and realize our chain is rusted out in a lot more places than we can count. If leadership starts at the top, at least two people should have been fired by now, if not three if we include Trump. Christopher Wray is the man at the top of the FBI, so he should have been the first to go, along with whoever received the information from the callers and failed to pass it on from the bottom on up the chain of command. And believe me, it's not hard to find out.

Who received the call? (YOU) and who did you tell? (NOBODY) Really? (YEAH, YOU'RE FIRED) It's that simple… cause we really have to lay down the law and start firing people that perform incompetently in their jobs. What's the saying: "Once a liar, always a liar." and I don't mean to keep pulling quotes out, but if they perform incompetently TODAY... Then what's going to stop them from performing incompetently tomorrow? It's like what I was saying about our politicians, if they are being bought off TODAY, then what makes you think that they aren't going to be bought off tomorrow? What's the saying, "Once a cheater, always a cheater." I mean we have a three-strikes law for violent criminals, but we allow our politicians to sell us out an unlimited amount of times and still have a job. Lie to us an unlimited amount of times and still have a job. Hmph…

Better yet, and I don't like to use it, because it is a touchy subject but we all know that Deputy Scot Peterson was a coward and failed us by failing to save our kids, so we would never trust him again to stay in that position, or hire him to protect our kids again, ˝NO˝! The simple truth is (NO) we would never, ever, ever, hire him again, nor would we ever, ever, EVER, allow him to stay on the job. the truth is for whatever reason, he failed us. As an officer, he must engage an active shooter, yet he didn't. The crazy part. is he failed us and was allowed to resign with full benefits and his pension, so we the taxpayers will be paying him for the rest of his life, for his failure.

In any case, he won't never be an officer anywhere else ever again. We know Scot Peterson dropped the ball, but my thing is who is the FBI agent or, agents, that failed to catch the ball in the first place. Someone got a tip and they never followed up on it. It was so bad, they never even notified the Miami Field Office about this tip. I mean we would never hire Scot Peterson ever again, so why should we still employ this FBI agent or, agents who failed us, as well.

Then it goes back to what I was originally saying about our U.S. Congress cause they have been standing there, like Scot Peterson, with the pen – forever – and have failed to act on gun legislation – forever – which would have prevented a lot of these mass shootings years ago. We have so many failures in our system that we have to start firing these people. If politicians in Congress are unwilling to stand up and stop taking money from these Lobbyist groups that's been meddling in our elections for years we should fire them. If we have to fire them all, we must fire them all and to be honest, *I'm calling on the American people to fire them all.* Again, how do we fire them all, don't vote for none of them, that's how we fire them all. If we want this madness to stop then we would be smart to end it by getting rid of them. They are the ones that's producing all of this madness and they are the ones that's keeping it going, so we help them out by keeping it going right out the door with them. And please close the door behind them! Problem solved, madness gone and then maybe we can get what we need and what we want. I mean at some point we have to face reality, face-to-face and end their fate in our government fast cause technically, it's all their fault.

I'm going to be serious and tell you we have to quit monkeying around and do a complete overhaul of our entire political system, and now. I know a lot of people think we just need to fine tune it, but at this point the corrosion is so caked-up that at this point it won't ever run like the fine oiled machine it was intended to. And that's

Okay! The quicker we realize it, the better off we are going to be. I mean we have overlooked it for so long, that we can't keep neglecting our own needs. If this was a marriage we'd end it – especially since they've admitted to our face to being in bed with the Lobbyist's

Like I say, – it would be retarded for us to think that they are working for us when we know they are on the Lobbyist's payroll for 10 times more. I'm sorry to tell you, but if we allow them to continue to make decisions for us we are going to come away empty handed every single time. I don't know about you, but I'm tired of walking away empty handed and not only that, but dumb-founded and disappointed as well. I can see if we were having, like, a minor discrepancy, but this has been a freaking major catastrophe. It's to the point that we can't even trust our government. This Trump administration is really dishonest and has no problem of lying, cheating, defrauding, and deceiving us. For that reason, I feel that they have lost their sense of honor and respect to the point that they are dishonorable and what we need to do is give them a dishonorable discharge and send them on their way.

Then we can come back around full circle to this FBI incompetence issue and continuously demand that somebody be held accountable here, especially, since this shooting was preventable on their level as well. There were so many red flags that our local, state, and federal governments missed and if we don't do something about it now what's to say they're not going to miss it again next time.

I mean recently too. We look at the FBI and we see all kinds of scandals from Jim Comey (once the head of the FBI) meddling in our elections, to Jim Comey admitting to leaking government information. We have him investigating leaking e-mails when he's the one leaking them (Yeah, Okay). Then we don't know whom to believe, the Republicans Nunes memo, or the Democrats memo, but even if we want to split it down the middle, we can say it was a 50/50 chance that the 'FBI and DOJ abused the FISA court, so now we have a preponderance of evidence that both the FBI and DOJ were, illegally wiretapping people. (Nixon was disgraced for that!) Then, our government can't even agree on that, like, are they doing it (Yes or No)? We can't even get a straight answer out of these people. Where is their accountability? I mean Trump was so busy calling these NFL players SOB's and how they were unpatriotic for not standing for the flag but look how unpatriotic he is by lying to us every single day. They want us, *We the People*, to stand up and respect the flag and respect the Country, but they're the ones that disrespect our flag. They not only disrespect our Country, but us as well for lying to us. I mean Trump went so far that he even admitted that he likes to keep our Country in chaos and conflict. Of course, all Trump supporters claim it was a joke, but like I said about his sexual assault/harassment case... it would be a joke if he wasn't doing what he admitted to doing. To me, if he didn't keep chaos and conflict, not only going on here in America, but all around the world, So Yeah, I believe at some point the Russians are laughing at us, laughing at how we actually voted a moron in as our President. Laughing at how our White House then turned into a daddy-daycare, or better yet, how a Country of 325 Million continuously allow less than 600, bought-off government officials to make all of these decisions which are thoroughly – corrupted. To tell you the truth I almost want to laugh myself, just to keep from crying, cause – it's true. The crazy part is it's not even like our politicians are even being discreet about it. They have gotten so comfortable with it that they just do it out in the open. Look at Senator Marco Rubio, in a building full of people and on National TV admitting that he's been paid millions of dollars by the NRA and is going to keep collecting a check as long as they are willing to pay. I mean, he said it with no remorse, nor was he apologetic.

In so many ways and words, he admitted on National TV to selling us out to the NRA. They have had their hands in the cookie jar so long that they don't even hide when they speak anymore. Then like I said, it would be different if they were getting paid and voting a different way, but they are voting the way they are getting paid. These Lobbyist are paying them to do deeds for them and they are. They are paying these politicians to look the other way and every time we look – they are. To make a long story short, they are doing exactly what the Lobbyist are paying them to do. The problem is they are supposed to do what *We the People* are paying them to do. Like I say, if you are taking money from the NRA you're condoning this. To me you're either part of the solution or part of the problem, especially since you see they don't even want to implement common-sense gun solutions. *WOW! Like really???*

I will say this about the FBI though, they did come out and admit that they failed to investigate the tips about Nikolas Cruz. It is a little more than I can say about Trump and Congress, or the Deputy (Coward) Scot Peterson. But while they did take the heat that still doesn't get them out the kitchen, we still have got to get down to who failed us and fire them. I'm not even interested in why it happened, I'm just interested in who; cause why is nothing more than an excuse or a lie and to me – both are useless. They claim that the House Judiciary Committee, is going to investigate the FBI, so maybe we can call on the FBI to investigate the House Judiciary Committee as well, so we can have them dig up dirt on each other. Play them against each other and at the end fire them both. Kill two birds with one stone. Probably even three cause we'll tell them to tell on someone else and we'll give them a plea bargain. As soon as they tell, and it's corroborated we'll laugh at them and flip flop on the deal like they do us. "But you said, "Tell on three and you'll let me go free?" Yeah, well, we lied! We learned it from you though!! Worked, didn't it? Yeah, sure isn't no fun when the rabbit got the gun, huh?

For real… that's how we got to do them until they all tell on each other and then we fire them all anyway. As for the FBI failure what can we say but we want someone's head to roll on this one. I don't mean to use that terminology here cause this issue is serious, so for those who don't know, it's just a phrase used about firing someone. Well, all I can say at the end of the day is that it was a fundamental lack of leadership in our local, state, and federal governments whom allowed this to happen. This horrible, foreseeable tragedy. We must strengthen our chain of command cause we can't afford allowing this to happen. We must, we must…

MARCH FOR OUR LIVES!!!

MARCH FOR OUR LIVES!!!

WE ARE CALLING B.S.!
WE ARE CALLING B.S.!
WE ARE CALLING B.S.!

-MSDHS

Gina Montalto

Here in America we are less than 5% of the world's population yet *We the People* hold close to 50% of all civilian firearms in the world. Therefore, there are more guns on our streets and in our homes than half of the People have around the world. Knowing that fact I'm calling B.S. on our government for its complete failure to step in and regulate this epidemic gun proportion we have going on here in America.

We have had school shootings and more school shootings than probably any other country on the globe and for that reason I'm calling B.S. Our government has failed to protect our kids in a manner no different than what's going on in Nigeria where the Boko Haram terrorist group kidnaped over 300 little girls in the town of Chibok and over 100 of them still remain in captivity. That was a tragic and horrific situation where these bustards went in and stole kids from school. Till this day they still hold up signs that read: #BRING OUR GIRLS BACK! To make my point if once wasn't enough, the Nigerian government inadequately and incompetently failed the kids there again! Just earlier this year in 2018 the Nigerian government dropped the ball again and allowed this heinous rebel group Boko Haram to kidnap 110 more girls from school in the town of Dapchi.

Just heartbreaking! The Nigerian government inconceivably allowed these ruthless militants to do it again. To me this is just incomprehensible about how they can be that careless when it comes to kid's safety at school. Losing the first 300 kids was unforgettable and now losing 110 more is unforgivable. I mean this was just disastrous and being a father with girls of my own, my heart just goes out to these kids, their parents, family, friends and for all of us that care about these kids in the world. We have failed them and *We the People* of the World have let them get brutally kidnaped, raped, tortured and sold into slavery, if not murdered.

Then we turn our attention to what's going on closer here at home and we see that we have allowed the same thing to happen to our own kids, that have gotten brutally murdered at school yet again. This has happened over and over again, and our federal government has not done nothing about it, even though they could have. We really need to take a hard look at ourselves in the mirror and call it for what it is... B.S. We can look at the Cleveland Elementary

School shooting in Stockton California some 34 years ago and then fast forward to this Marjory Stoneman Douglas High School shooting in 2018 and ask ourselves *why* wasn't something done then and most importantly *why* wasn't the first school shooting the last school shooting? For that reason, I'm calling B.S. For over 34 years our federal government has known that these shootings have been going on and they have failed to protect our kids, no differently than the Nigerian government has failed the kids there. Our federal government would probably say it's different, but if they did... forget calling B.S... I'm screaming B.S... because that's what this screams B.S., B.S., B.S.!!!

You know how I know this is all B.S., because in 1996, when the country of Australia had a mass shooting in Port Author that left 35 people dead there, they immediately implemented a series of gun laws and ever since then the gun violence plummeted in that country. The same with the United Kingdom when they had a similar mass shooting incident that left many dead, they too immediately implemented a series of gun laws that has worked to prevent these mass shootings. I mean we can look at Canada to the North and when they had a series of mass shootings they did the same as well, so **the problem can be rectified** but our federal government is so lame, moronic and/or sellouts that they haven't done nothing to fix our problem here at home. For that I'm calling B.S.

Here in America we have had shooting after shooting after shooting. If it's not a school – it's a church and if it's not a church – it's a concert and if it's not a concert – it's someone's home and we can't get our own government to take action. Like I say... even if implementing stricter gun laws saved one life it would be well worth it, but to no avail our federal government obviously doesn't care. This has been going on for years and yet they've done nothing. We have had more school shooting than I dare to count. We have had church shooting after church shooting and every other mass shooting from movie theaters, to malls, to again concerts and nightclubs, that again I don't dare to count. We have also had countless shootings on our streets and even at our very own military bases and yet our federal government has failed to act in any manner whatsoever. For that reason, I'm calling B.S.

We have states going in all different directions on gun laws trying to do something to rectify our problem, but since the states can't agree on one consistent law then it's all pointless. It's like Walmart and Dick's Sporting Goods not selling firearms anymore, but the gun show is still going on with the gun show loopholes and relaxed background checks right next door in the next parking lot, and the fact that we can't get our federal government to implement one consistent law across the board is B.S. Right now, TODAY, we have over 227.5 Million People in America calling for stricter federal gun reform and our federal government of less than 600 People have pretty much said "NO" they are not going to do much of anything about it and if they did, it's not going to be near enough of what we need at this time. For that reason, I'm calling B.S.

I know we call on our law enforcement officers to protect us, but they can only do so much and at times can barely protect themselves, so our lawmakers need to do their job in order to protect all of us. I'm sorry... but we have had enough talk for a lifetime over these mass shootings to the point that I'm sick and tired of it and for that reason I'm calling B.S. The time for talking is over and *We the People* must not just start demanding action but must demand action TODAY. We simply have to do something different cause nothing has changed, and nothing will change unless we put our foot down and demand action TODAY. We have to put our kids first, just like Australia, the U.K. and Canada did. I know everyone wants to point the finger at the local police or the FBI for dropping the ball, but the real finger must be pointed at our federal government because they haven't thrown us more or less a catchable ball – if that makes sense. Not saying that we don't have to demand action on all fronts to stop this problem cause fault does lay in our state and local police, as well as our federal investigators, but it is our federal government that lays down the laws and do more. They have no reason for their inaction other than being bought off and for that reason I'm really calling B.S.

If everyone knows that real change starts at the top, then gee-by-golly-willikers… *We the People* must demand immediate action at the top and the ones at the top is our federal government. If 227.5 Million People here in America want our federal government to mandate stricter gun control laws, then *We the People* should have stricter gun control laws, and their refusal to do so is going against what *We the People* want. At this point this is no longer a Democracy, but some type of communist regime. I see no other way around that other than to say what they're doing is treasonous to us – the American People. We ask them to do something and not only do they not do it, but they are accepting money for not doing it. That's why we must do what our very own kids have said already and that is**… if our government officials are not going to work for us then we need to vote them out and elect people that are going to represent us…** cause at this point we are getting screwed over. It's like our current elected officials have forgotten that *We the People* still run this country and that's why we live in a democratic society, but we stand up and demand action cause our federal government is obviously not living up to our democratic standards of reality. Let's be honest and admit that our federal government, for whatever reason it be, have not taken us seriously. They have outright ignored or refused our every request for change which only proves my point that they have no empathy, no sympathy and obviously no compassion for our kid's safety or our own. Am I missing something or does this sound communistic? I'm pretty sure if *We the People* wanted a communistic society we would elect one, but I'm telling you – I'm with the kids and calling freaking B.S. cause what our federal government has been doing has really been treasonous to us – the American people.

I do get that it's not all of them because we have had people like Nancy Pelosi stand up there for hours trying to get our point across the floor for the dreamers and other senators like Chuck Schumer who have tried to put a plan together for the DACA kids, as well, but leave it to Trump and many Republicans in congress and *We the People* can't get a deal on these DACA kids that a polling of over 70% of Americans want to happen. That's why Trump's approval rating is only around 30% because he only does what 30% of the county wants him to do and I'm sorry… in a democracy it doesn't work that way. In a democracy, the majority rules and *We the People* must decide what the majority wants and demand that they rule that way or else… Point Blank Period.

To be honest, I'm sick and tired of going up and down and up and down on this wicked roller coaster ride our federal government has us on. I'm going to be the first to admit that it didn't just start with this Trump administration, but they sure have taken it and speeded it up to the point that I'm sick. I just want off! To make this roller coaster more of an analogy to our current point on gun control, we have told them to stop all of the loopholes on everything they do from special interest to closing the gun show loop holes and they won't stop it. They obviously think it's funny… but it's not. We have a president that goes golfing when our country is mourning the loss of and burying our kids. Really looking at it for what it is, this shouldn't come at much of a surprise from Trump and this administration who has threatened to totally annihilate places like

N. Korea which would have instantly killed an estimated 3 Million innocent women and kids from N. Korea to S. Korea to Japan and probably Guam as well. And trust and believe that if they could have pushed the button… and the world turned a blind eye and they could get away with it… they would have done it already. To me, honestly, Trump's mind is like a maniac serial killer who doesn't bat an eyelash to blowing up 3 Million people or mind playing golf when our country is mourning the loss of our kids. That's why they don't care about doing gun reform, *for real*! For the life of me I don't see how we were in the middle of a Constitutional crisis of gun violence here in America where *We the People* were seeking action and our leader in charge goes golfing. For that reason, I'm calling B.S.

For crying out loud, these are our children we are talking about and we can't get our president and federal government to lay down common-sense gun laws that will protect them and us too. *Where is the real leadership in that?* We not only have our kids being shot in schools, but we have people being murdered in church and our federal government officials are still in the business of taking money from the NRA to turn a blind eye to all of this. The South Carolina church shooting happened a couple years back and even as of late we had the Texas church shooting and the worst mass shooting in modern day history with the Las Vegas massacre and we still can't get our federal government to implement adequate background checks on the purchases of firearms that based on facts may have prevented the church shootings and the Pulse Nightclub shooting. Not to mention that had they done their job… and banned the sale of bump stocks… that they know have illegally turned these semi-automatic firearms into illegal machine guns… we may have had less casualties in the Las Vegas massacre. The most trying part is that the only reason they haven't implemented these common-sense guns laws is based on nothing but greed. Cause if they did so it's common-sense to assume... the NRA won't cut them these million dollar checks anymore, period. *We are losing our kids' lives based on their greed!*

I guess the saying is true, that it's easier for a camel to go through the eye of a needle, than for a rich man to enter into the kingdom of God, cause it is undisputed that our state and federal government has both sold us all out for money. For that reason, I'm Calling B.S. We have Trump who claims he wants to be president for all the People but refusing to act on 70% of the American People's reasonable requests for comprehensive gun reform all because he doesn't want to stop his NRA check or upset his base, is absurdity. Maybe if he did what 70% of the People wanted done in this country, instead of the 30%, he would have a 70% approval rating, but I guess he's too dumb to figure that out or he loves living in a communistic society where the majority of the People don't rule the nation. To make my point, this has almost been a shut up and do as they say so ordeal instead of *We the People* asking. We must start demanding and if we don't get what we want then we already know we must vote them out.

The time to act is right here and right now and if the GOP Congress don't act for us for whatever reason, then in the name of keeping our kids and communities safe from gun violence we should have no problem voting them out in this 2018 mid-term election. I'm telling you if they don't fix this now and *We the People* don't vote them out then, I'm telling you right now I'm screaming B.S. on all of us – the American People. We must do something cause it's like our MSDHS kids said: "*Why* go back to school where we're just sitting ducks and they can't protect us." This was the deadliest school shooting since Sandy Hook and we should have demanded our federal government implement every method available to end the gun violence then, yet we are still sitting here asking for common-sense gun laws now. That does not make no sense and the crazy part is they shouldn't be allowed to make cents when this doesn't make sense, if that makes any sense? This is really a Republican issue and it is the majority of Republicans that have been getting paid to turn a blind eye on this issue, so since the Republicans control the White House and the Congress then we must demand that they stop taking NRA change and start making some change TODAY. Or like I said, we really have to start making some change ourselves and vote these People out.

Right now, they have the unlimited power to act and we can't even rely on them to act in our best interest. Our kids have cried out in the streets with an emotional plea for help **and** over 70% of *We the People* have sent our federal government an S. O.S. "Save Our Student" message, yet we can't get an adequate response from our government on this issue. This lack of ethical leadership is what's been ruining our nation and for that reason I'm calling B.S. We just lost 14 students and 3 teachers. And almost lost the real hero, Anthony Borges who was wounded the worst saving others. *We the People* have to fight for them! Their refusal to serve and protect us all has gone past mere negligence too deliberate indifference cause they've known of this serious gun violence epidemic and have done nothing to stymie it. This is not only unreasonable, but it's callous and for that reason I'm calling B.S.

Our government has an individual responsibility to take care of our safety and they have constantly kicked the can down the road even as people lay in the streets dead. Now we must show them that they kicked the wrong can... this time they kicked the can with the hornets' nest and we are going to keep stinging them until we get action, or we run them off. Here, the Florida legislature has attempted to calm their stinging by implementing some gun safety measures, but they have not gone far enough to ensure our safety.

Apparently, they signed into legislation the ban of bump stocks, raised the minimum purchasing age to buy a firearm to 21, implemented a 3-day waiting period on the purchase of all firearms and gave law enforcement more authority to seize weapons when someone appears mentally unfit, but again that's simply not far enough. Especially when we must ban the sale of all assault weapons and limit the capacity of all gun magazine clips – that – will ensure a lot more safety.

In that Florida Bill they also passed what they call a Guardian Program that would allow voluntary teachers to be armed in schools, but even the Florida Teachers Union is calling on the Governor of Florida Rick Scott to veto that measure by stating: "Teachers should not have to choose between confronting a gunmen and getting their students to safety" I guess this was the idiotic Donald Trump's version where he adamantly called to arm our teachers, but I guess in doing so they recently missed the news where the teacher recently fired shots in the classroom in Dalton? Yeah, just arm the teachers why don't you?? Then the only reason why they're even talking about arming the teachers is because they want to be cheapskates instead of hiring some of our real trained military personnel that's served in their wars (not ours) to protect our kids. They can pass a tax plan to give 1.5 Trillion dollars in tax breaks to these already super rich Wall Street Corporations, but they don't want to pay to protect our kids in school? How about this, we send their armed guards that's protecting them in the White House and in Congress to our schools and we send our teachers to protect them and we'll see how they feel about that? Yeah, that's what I thought, so they need to give us a break cause I'm tired of calling B.S. already, but you know what, I don't give a damn I'm still calling B.S.!!!

This is not a game and if their looking for an inexpensive fix then instead of keeping our military on our bases, they can deploy them to do combat missions at our schools. We have a lot of people that join our military (male and female) and that would be a great military job of protecting our kids for them. To make my point, we have so many options, but our problem is our government don't care to come up with any viable ideas cause they are so freaking dumb that they don't have any. They don't even want to use common-sense gun laws that's already proven to work. That's why I say let's be honest with ourselves and admit that our federal government is not reflecting the views of the 70% of the American People that want stricter gun laws by refusing to set the tone at the top. That's why they say admittance leads to acceptance cause once we admit and accept that they are not for us then we don't have to call B.S. on them no more, we can call it for what it is... B.S. on ourselves *for failing to get rid of them.* (Just saying!)

A lot of people may or may not want to accept the fact that our government has failed us, but like the MSDHS kids told them already: "If you supported us you would change it now", and what did they do... (NOTHING)! At least let's be honest and admit that it was nothing of substance and we can't continue to stand by and let them get away with doing nothing. Nothing just don't work when we really need a whole lot of something! So... we really need to sit down and call it for what it is B.S.!!! Cause I really do believe the fact checkers when they say the Trump administration has lied to us over 2000 times in their first year in office. I believe that and I'm sorry... but 2000 lies in 365 days is a lot of freaking lies. I don't even dare do the math on that, but I could only imagine that that equates to about 6.66 lies per day. Lying that much, you got to be of the devil. (I don't know about you... but my parents would have whipped that devil right out of me!) I mean it's so many lies that it just sounds unbelievable! But I'm here to tell you folks that that number is not FAKE NEWS. Especially when you have people like

Hope Hicks coming forward and admitting that she sometimes tells little white lies for Trump. Well I'll tell you what, the saying by William Paley says: "White lies always produce others of a darker complexion" so yeah, they have been lying to us from day one. I honestly don't believe nothing they say. If they're not flat out lying to us, then we're getting half-truths, or a spin on the truth or else some kind of flip flop on what they said they were going to do but didn't. So, for them to say they are going to fix this issue, I'm sorry to say it, but history has proven otherwise.

One thing for sure, with the forthcoming of Hope Hicks testimony we truthfully know that Donald Trump expects his staff to lie to us and he berates them and fires them when they no longer want too. Honestly, that's why we are 5 communication Directors and 2000 lies later with this Trump Administration, (just saying!) I guess that if you want a friend in the political realm of Washington, D.C., you go buy a dog cause you just can't trust none of them to be loyal and tell you the truth! What's the saying: "Tell the truth and shame the devil!" Well I'll tell you what… They must be praising the devil cause we literally have kids dying in our schools and on our streets and Washington is literally bought off by the NRA to do anything about it. For real, they're probably too busy selling us out so they can get money for their 666 building in New York that his son-in-law Kushner is in debt over a Billion Dollars for. You think I'm playing, but I will tell you this for sure, you can't worship God on one hand and take the money to snub the kids and everyone else on the other. It just doesn't work that way and now we are back to that awkward moment of that all aboard GOP train accident. Yeah, holy cow huh???

I mean they can talk out the side of their necks all they want too but talking is one thing and doing is another. The crazy part is everybody on the planets watching and they haven't even started

doing nothing. What's the saying: "Shit or get off the pot" please…
I now know why people came up with all of these sayings cause it
just fits these people perfectly. Well I better throw in the saying that
"there's no fool like an old fool" cause that saying just fits Trump to
the T. Not to mention he's out of touch with reality and clearly not
only has he flown over the Cuckoo's nest, but over the whole damn
hill as well!

Y'all think I'm playing, but Trump is such a psychopath that in
the beginning he made this school massacre all about him. In an
attempt to attack the Mueller investigation by claiming that the FBI
was "too busily focused on the Russia collusion thing to stop the
gunmen" in this situation. How sadistic is that? Then he had the
nerve to call the FBI disgusting, but I guess he should have looked
in the mirror before he used the death of these children to spin it
back towards him in what was nothing more than another bad joke.
Trump knows that the Mueller investigation has at most 35 people
working on that investigation and he has over 35,000 people
working for him in the FBI, so for Trump to even throw that B.S. as
a joke out there like that I'm calling B.S.! If anything, he's the
freaking bad joke that's disgusting for not only playing golf amidst
this school shooting when we are laying kids to rest near his
compound, but for taking money to turn a blind eye on this gun issue
to begin with. For that reason, I'm calling B.S.

There is so much more, but before I move on I just want to call
B.S. on MSDHS Resource Officer Scot Peterson. First, he claimed
that he thought he heard firecrackers, but an AR-15 doesn't sound
nothing like a firecracker and even worse he claimed that he thought
the gunshots were coming from outside the school building.
However, according to Sherriff Israel who reviewed the school's
camera showed this coward standing at the freaking door with his
gun out listening to the shooting and screaming going on in this

building for 4 freaking minutes and did nothing. And he was wearing a bullet proof vest! Yeah, the teacher needed that who jumped in front of those kids to save them, not this coward! Then not to mention the other 3 deputies the school cameras showed later standing outside the door and for that reason I'm calling B.S… "Bull-Shit" on all of them and the FBI agents that dropped the ball. Cause that's what this is B.S. and we need to stand up to these cowards and against our government cause they are not our friends, so we can make sure that this doesn't happen Never Again… Yup…

MARCH FOR OUR LIVES!!!

Sell us OUT
And We'll VOTE YOU OUT

Joaquin Oliver

O ur government allowed this shooter Nikolas Cruz to purchase 10 rifles. He was only 19 years old, and my question is: *"How in the heck was a 19-year-old allowed to legally purchase 10 firearms?"* Even if he was a 30-year-old there should still be a limit on how many guns a person can legally purchase before it becomes excess. This is insane to allow these people to stock pile so many weapons. Especially weapons that are made for nothing more than killing humans. Hadn't we learned that from Stephen Paddock in the Las Vegas Shooting where he was allowed to purchase an unlimited amount of assault rifles and then he used them to our demise without having to do much reloading at all. 58 dead and over 500 wounded and all our government did was offer thoughts, prayers and condolences.

In this case I guess the families of the 58 slain will receive $275,000 dollars and the remainder will be distributed to the wounded, but to me that would only be a slap in the face. There is no amount of money that they could pay me to make me feel any better. If anything, this is a 'take this money and go buy out the bar' where I would be left to wallow in my own misery money. All while our president continues to play golf – with no intention of doing a damn thing about it. A lot of Republicans ask why many people want to see Trump fail as president, but I just can't see how they don't see that he's failing us – the American People. He doesn't do nothing and have watched us bury our kids and still has no real intention on doing anything about it, except go play golf which I'm willing to bet he sucks at cause he sucks at everything else. My bad… Stupid me… I forgot… he is really good at some things…. Lying, cheating, being an all-around scumbag, need I go on... yeah, you already know don't you! (Ha-ha)

You see what I am most troubled about and most upset about is instead of playing golf he should have been in the Oval Office burning the midnight oil, trying to figure out a solution to all this madness, but yet he's at his resort retreat spending the money he received from the NRA to turn his back on this very issue.

And you know what, I'm sorry… because I can't help but to berate these people. The more and more I think about it, berating them is the only thing that comes even close to allowing me to release my frustration. Maybe it's the putting my thoughts on paper that makes me feel better. Talking to you about them instead of holding them inside. Then it is the shimmer of hope that these words will rabble rouse all of us, *We the People,* to really stand up and

March for Our Lives! It's like what Author Hugh Clough said: "Tis better to have fought and lost, then never to have fought at all", with that said it's better to have Marched for Our Lives then to have Marched at all. Win lose or draw, we're trying and at the end of the day, sometimes that's what counts the most. To me it's better to go down fighting then to sit here outraged and dishonored.

If it's true that the pen is mightier than the sword, then I must put it to war with paper. I'll tell you what, if it is to mimic a gun, to say the least it has been smoking! I will tell you this though and I believe Abraham Lincoln said it the best when he said: "The ballot is much stronger than the bullet". We have to hit them where it hurts and that is at the ballot box. To further quote Abraham Lincoln again in that if "a house divided against itself cannot stand", then we the 70% of the majority must tear it down and build a new one that's built to last. If *We the People* of America can build Ford tough, then *We the People* can build our fortress tougher. Right now, we have to look before taking shelter under the fortress we have, because come to find out – it's just a shabby den full of wolves and they have no intentions of protecting us – the sheep, if that makes sense.

TODAY, we have met our new enemy in this country and they are our very own politicians. They have preyed on us like vampires sucking the blood out of us and it's time to use our one silver bullet at the ballot box. It's time to bring what they have done in the dark to light, so they can perish. Like T.I., the rapper, said in one of his songs "If God is with us who can be against us... they can't make us suffer, just make us tougher, motivation". That's what we need right now is motivation more than anything. If money is the motivator, then I'm sorry... I'm broke. But to give you words of encouragement to get you motivated I would say just remember that the spoils of war go to the victor and the spoils in this case is your life, your liberty and your own pursuit of happiness. You know what people try to tell me all the time is "Griffin you got a lot of game" and that's cause life to me is serious. This is not a game. Kids losing their lives should never ever be taken by our government so lightly. To be honest, I have been appalled at how ridiculously desensitized our nation leaders have been on this issue and then that's why we're back to the point we can't get nothing done cause… they simply… "JUST DON'T CARE". The only thing they care about is selling us out to the highest bidder and that's why I say if they continuously sell us out we got to vote them out. Shout it loudly… "SELL US OUT AND WE'LL VOTE YOU OUT"! And I'm sorry, I don't know about you, but I feel they already sold me out when they sold these kids out by taking NRA money and not doing a dang thing about our gun epidemic problem. Now I'm ready to vote them all out and sow new seeds for you, me and our kids to be free from all of this turmoil, extreme confusion and chaos that we see.

This is crazy, and we have got to be insane to continuously allow this craziness to occur. We got to stand up and demand that they get up off their lazy asses onto their dying feet and doing something or else we won't never get nothing done. They try to say the squeaky wheel doesn't get the grease, but I'll tell you what, it can! *We the People* just have to be the squeaky wheel that won't go away until we get what we want. Otherwise, we'll be sitting in ruins. Do you know that a new day is on the horizon? We got to get out there and meet our destiny head on. The time for waiting is over, especially since we know that victory awaits those who have everything in order. Like Franklin D. Roosevelt said himself: "The only thing to fear is fear itself" so we shall not be afraid of our politicians or the NRA. We are the American People and we run this country and we will fight for what we believe in! It's like Patrick Henry said: "give me liberty or give me death" and I'm going to finish that statement and say we will win if we have to do it all ourselves.

We are the American People and we must band together like never before cause if we don't we are going to continue to face trouble with this mass shooting epidemic like never before. We have to go out on a limb and face our fears cause not facing our fears is only going to keep us in trouble. Once we step from under that umbrella of fear we will get the change we most desperately seek and that is our own safety and security. What's the saying "We reap what we sow, that's how it goes". Well we have to sow seeds of morality, honesty and integrity with ourselves and that's what we will reap from everyone around us. Our government treats us bad only because we allow them too, but if we fire them all and take back our power, we will have the country we all so desperately desire. Like I said, we are a nation of over 300 Million People and we allow roughly 600 people (most of them imbeciles) in our federal government to wreak havoc in our lives. We have Trump that even admits to liking chaos and confusion, so what do you think we are going to get in our lives if we keep him in charge? (Yes, chaos and confusion)!

I believe it was George Washington who told us years ago that a "two-party system won't work" here in America. It's like the Bible says, "You will either like one master and hate the other", something like that... but what I'm saying is we will only continue to fight amongst each other if we don't come together for our own greater good. Anything other than that and we won't never get nothing done. As Theodore Roosevelt once said: "There can be no fifty-fifty Americanism in this country. There is room here for only one hundred percent Americanism." We are sitting here fighting each other and I'm pretty sure we will find that 100% of our rational minds here in America want to keep our kids and ourselves safe. I mean, even as it stands we are already at 70% in favor of stricter gun laws and don't worry the other 30 % are morons cause how do you not vote for stricter gun laws… To tell you the truth, those must be the remaining Trump supporters that just don't care about none of us. The crazy part is, we have a 70% majority wanting stricter gun laws and we still can't get them passed through Congress.

We have a serious problem here in America and it starts with us Americans. I say that because if we don't come together and change within, our outer world will never change around us, except for maybe worse.

We can keep playing around or we can go ahead and get it right. They say it's best to do it one time correctly, then to rush and have to do it all over again. I am a firm believer of getting it done right the first time. In this regard, we just want our federal government to get the ball rolling in the right direction on the right issues. When we find out it's not 100% later we will fix it. At this point I am mentally and physically fatigued, but I will not stop because I set out with a goal in mind to write and publish this book and I won't stop until I see it through. My grammar might be off, but hey, I did it and to me that's what counts the most. I won't quit until I've reached my goal. That's why I'm saying that we shall not quit on our kids until we meet their goal and that is **safety first** in all aspects. We literally have to come up with a plan to keep us safe. If we leave it to the politicians of this country they're going to sell us out every time. Therefore, we must stop asking for action and demand action nonstop, until we get action. We must implement a plan and see it through till the end... till we win... It's called victory and we shall be victorious! It can also be called success and the same thing applies as we shall be the successors. I always look at it as we can't stop, won't stop until the job gets done. Like Jason Aldean says, "that's the only way I know"!

So, all I can say is let's get it done before someone else dies. Otherwise, we will be left here asking ourselves *why* we didn't do more! I guess it's like a great coach would say "leave it all on the floor" or "Tall on the field". We have to leave it all on ourselves to get adequate gun reform through Congress TODAY. I know everyone has expectations of what gun legislation should look like. I know the expectations bar should be high. If the bar is high, security and sanity should be priorities, but if our expectation is low, then let us raise the bar higher. For our safety, we need to be raising it towards outer space cause when it comes to our life, liberty and pursuit of happiness, the sky should be the limit. If they push against us, we shall push back harder cause in the end we will not be deprived. America didn't get to be the land of the free, if it wasn't for all of us – the brave! Now since we are no longer the land of the weak and the home of the slave, we must stand up to our government cause they really are starting to act like this is a communist kind of thing. For whatever reason our government thinks we work for them, but you know what, they work for us and we got to remind them of that. *We the People* are the ones in charge and if 70% of us want stricter gun laws then *We the People* get stricter gun laws and it's time that we flex our vote and show them who's boss. I'm just hoping we can really get the GOP donors to really put their money where their hearts are and not support the GOP party until we get a ban again on these killing machine assault rifles and our gun legislation through Congress.

Trust and believe many GOP see what's happening to our kids and how they are making a desperate plea for action, so hopefully they really get in on the action and help us get some action or demand the GOP party take action. *We the People* no matter what party affiliation have to hold our politicians accountable, especially since this Trump administration and Congress is so dysfunctional. If our future depends on what we do TODAY, then we must start TODAY, or to say the very least, we would be blind, deaf and dumb not too. We can't be naive to the fact that our government has taken advantage of us cause we are getting screwed at every turn. From inadequate action on comprehensive gun legislation to inadequate attention on medical and mental health treatment. We have a failure at our federal level at all the major fronts that we face as a nation. Quite frankly I'm sick and tired of hearing their weak and pathetic explanations. We have depended on them to get it right and they simply can't. The stock market may be at an all-time high, but first there's not many Americans that have money in the Stock market beyond 401Ks and second, we don't give a damn about the money – we want to go after the NRA. At the end of the day, money is just money and we can't take it with us when we die, nor can we spend it unless we are still alive, so we just want to be protected first and then we will worry about the money. *I mean does that sound fair*, cause we have asked those that we put in charge to change gun laws and they act like they don't hear us. I guess once they get in charge they no longer speak our language? I know my grammar may not be the best, but it's comprehendible. Everything they've been doing is simply inconceivable.

Our politicians are pretty much just puppets that waste our taxpayer dollars while doing nothing. Our president has been under investigation for collusion, obstruction of justice and sexual misconduct allegations from the beginning. Trump's currently under fire for paying to play with play girls, play models and every single thing else in between. Every day I wake up and think this is who we have in charge? Shoot… no wonder why we can't get anything done. He's a real crook. To say the least, he has not risen one bit to meet our American idealism, nor does he have the moral or ethical capacity to do the job as president. Not to mention that his intelligence is mindless, and his freaking tweets are needless. It's a shame to see how lost he really is. He doesn't even know that meddling and collusion are two different things. We have really given him a pass by lowering our expectations cause we know he's insane. Seriously though, we should not stand by and have OUR high standards of excellence stooped to such a low, like it has under this Trump administration. I'm going to be honest and say that our previous Obama, W. Bush and Clinton administrations were bad, but with this Trump administration we have just jumped out the frying pan and directly into the flames. (Make it stop already!) All we want is stricter gun laws, *is that too much to ask for? Or the expectation to keep us safe?*

Leave it to Trump we are not going to get jack. He has literally wreaked havoc everywhere and publicly shamed us all over the world. We honestly can't trust him as far as we can throw him. Our Vice President Mike Pence is nowhere to be found. Rex Tillerson, the one I was really leaning on is now gone, so the madness is only getting worse. I just really hope the Republicans are really re-thinking their position on Trump. I know their whole mantra is to unify the party behind anybody, but if I was them I would want to be a part of an amazing party, not a chaotic party. I know a person joins a party for the like mindedness of their constituents, but anyone that has a like mind like Trump, OMG! Trump has no morals or values and to support that means...? I know a lot of People say they like that Trump shows up and give speeches, but they must know that he's just reading, and the crazy part is… he probably didn't even write one word of it. He has some of the best speech writer's money can buy, we take them away and we are in for a crazy field day. Like what did he just say? The weirdest stuff ever has come out of his mouth and we see that all the time with his unfiltered tweets.

I mean everything about Trump is all bad, even to the point his temperament is unfit to be president. Believe me, I don't want to harp on Trump more than I have to, but I do so cause I know real change can only come from above. But then we look at how corrupt they are at the top and dare we begin to venture into looking at the bottom? This is disastrous and all we want is gun reform, so we can live, but we can't even get that!

I'm pretty sure a lot of people thought Trump the Billionaire was going to be the one to come in and change Washington, D.C., for the best, but let's be honest – he's not. They thought. he was going to offer us great advice, but let's be honest – he's not. I bet you they thought he was going to also give great suggestions, hire the best people and make the best recommendations – he's not. I'm going to say it like the saying says, "His two cents aren't even worth the copper they're minted on". It's fool's gold and Trumps playing us as the fool. We can't even get him to step-up and take a few lumps from his base. Better yet stand up, be a man, apologize, and be accountable, but waiting on that day is like waiting on hell to freeze over. As long as we got people in the world, like Trump, that won't never come to pass. But, that's why we got to quit giving him a pass because he doesn't care one bit about our ass. He only cares about himself and his bottom line and that's why we got to get rid of him this next election time.

I guess many Americans knew he had no experience in the political spectrum and many knew he didn't have the mental ability to do it. However, there were many Americans that hoped he would come in and be a Nick Foles. A Monday morning quarterback and win the Super Bowl, but in this scenario, we find out that he's a real Raider's Jamarcus Russell bust. For them the expectations may have been high, but now were just waiting here to see how low this fiasco is going to go. At this point to keep up with the NFL analogy... we are like the Cleveland Browns 0-16 back to back losing seasons and I'm left wondering how they would hire Hug Jackson on for another season. They must like losing, that's all I can say about it, 0-16...

twice! Maybe their thinking they're winning cause they are getting the draft pick every year, but I'm sorry... trading up to get the #1 pick is a success, tanking to get it is a disgrace.

Nonetheless, that's how I feel about Trump and Congress at this point cause they have been tanking for quite some time, and the #1 draft picks they allege they are choosing (Trump), are a bust. In theory we don't even need them cause they don't do nothing now. Therefore, they are a waste of tax payers dollars. They have been nothing but poor back seat driver's leading us in the wrong direction. The have left it to the lobbyist and the NRA to dictate most of our policy. What we need is real leadership cause we are getting nothing but the short end of the stick. With Trump, it's still coming with more commotion, disorder and fuss then I care to discuss. To me they have represented us so ineffectively that it's to the point of tyranny. This has absolutely turned into a taxation without representation situation. However, to make my point here at the end, we have to stand up and fight and...

MARCH FOR OUR LIVES!!!

MARCH FOR OUR LIVES!!!

CHAPTER 12

They're Going to hear us ROAR...

-Katy Perry

Alaina Petty

Louder, louder than the lion cause we are Americans and they are going to hear us ROOAAARRRRRR... The title of this Chapter is not a metaphor... It's meant literally. These kids and their supporters Marched on Washington, D.C. and they roared. Wasn't that something that the President was down at his resort in Mar-a-Lago playing golf, and the Vice President was missing in action too. All while our kids were Marching on Washington, D.C., on that Saturday, March 24, 2018. To say I was so pissed would be an understatement. I screamed louder, and my heart hurt worse for these kids.

The whole world really heard us roar. OMG... Those kids didn't just scream and holler and wave their signs. They got up there and gave speeches to massive crowds like the world has never seen before. Moms demanded action, dads demanded action, kids demanded action, and now, *We the People* are demanding action, TODAY! We are raising our fist in the air and waving our hands everywhere. We are waving everything but the white flag and demanding everything including the kitchen sink.

This is not a game and if they think we are going to go away, then they must think we are playing. I know one thing for sure, if we don't risk nothing, we are not going to get nothing and like Hellen Keller said: "Although the world is full of suffering, it is full also of overcoming it" Till this point we've suffered, till this point our kids and families have died and with their spirit we'll overcome it. No longer will we risk nothing and gain nothing. We have risked too much already and now we must gain everything. We will no longer be the outsiders in our Nation, we will be the infielders and we will be the winners. They want to feed us feathers – while they eat steak, they want to give us crumbs – while they eat the whole cake, but TODAY is the day we rise up and demand action. We shall March in our streets like they wouldn't believe and yell and scream, that we too, shall enjoy our American Dream.

We already had 17 kids staging a lay-in in Washington, D.C., and still they refuse to listen to the kids and they still refuse to listen you and me. If they are sleeping, our roar will wake them up; if they are dreaming, our roar will shake them up, and if they are deaf, then our signs will show them what we want. They got a loophole for everything, well we'll have a plan to plug each and every hole. Just in the past week I've been doing a lot of research into the second Amendment and I found out we are getting duped.

The District of Columbia, *which is Washington, D.C.*, prohibits the sale of assault weapons. They have gone so far to define assault weapons to include certain brands and models- of semi-automatic rifles pistols and shotguns; such as Colt AR-15 series rifles, as well as semi-automatic firearms with certain features, regardless of make, model, or safety features; such as semi-automatic rifles with 'pistol grips' which protrude conspicuously beneath the action of the weapon or a 'thumbhole stock'.

The District of Columbia also prohibits possession of "any large-capacity ammunition feeding devices, which includes magazines... or similar devices that have a capacity of more than 10 rounds of ammunition."

How crazy is that... they will ban the sale of assault rifles, bump stocks, and large-capacity magazines where they live, *in Washington, D.C.*, but they refuse to do it at home where you live. That's like saying, in the lower socio-economic communities they have liquor stores on every corner, but in the higher echelon communities, a liquor store with the words liquor on it can't be found anywhere in the community.

But wait there's more... *In Washington, D.C.*, you have to appear in person to disclose your information, name, address, occupation, and the details about your firearms. You have to show registration certificates and appear in person for the firearm to be registered. You have to show your ballistic identification (which means identify your bullets). They also do mandatory check-ups (which must be random checks) They don't allow more than one pistol to be registered in a 30-day period. There is also a vision requirement test, similar to one qualifying you for a driver's license.

When you appear in person with the firearm, you must demonstrate knowledge pertaining to all firearms and in particular proper, safe and responsible use, handling, and storage of the gun. You must get fingerprinted and photographed, and undergo a new background check every 6 years. On top of that you have to attend firearm training or safety courses providing "a total of at least one hour of firing training and a total of four hours of classroom training." If you don't believe me please go see, Heller v D.C., 670 F.3d 1244; cause that's the case I got all the information from.

However, the bizarre part is they would require all this near their home and their schools, but not yours. Near your home and schools, they refuse to implement any of it. They don't sell bump stocks *in Washington, D.C.,* assault rifles, or large-capacity magazines, but they will sell them in your community. Trust and believe the gun show loopholes and inadequate background checks only go on in your backyards, they don't go down *in Washington, D.C.* They made sure of that when it came to safety, they closed all of the loopholes in their town and shored up the background check system in their town, to where you got to even pass a vision requirement to be allowed to operate a firearm *in Washington, D.C.* Not to mention, you must pass a training and safety course. They demand that fingerprints and photographs are taken when an individual appears in person to register their firearms. To make a long story short, they have been short changing us from the very start.

They implement stringent laws for their safety and deregulate the entire system when it comes to ours. For that reason, I'm calling on you to call B.S. *They truly don't care about our lives!* You can think I'm playing this time or you can jump up and down, scream and shout, and let them hear us roar, because if they can ban assault rifles and other weapons of war in their home and in their stores, they can ban the sale of them in ours.

You know as I was reading this, Heller v D.C., case I couldn't believe my eyes, but then as I was done reading... you know what I really couldn't say that I was at all surprised. These days with our federal government, nothing seems to surprise me, maybe disgust me, but not surprise me. Therefore, I will tell you what... We all need to rise up and give them a little surprise when they realize how vast our March on Washington actually appears in their eyes. If Trump thought his inauguration crowd was huge, then gee-by-golly he's in for a ruse (or better yet a rude awakening) cause we are going to March on Washington, D.C. time and time again. Each and every time they are going to hear us Roar all the way around the world, just like the first time. If they won't sell assault weapons and high-capacity round magazines in Washington, D.C., then we must band together and demand that they not be allowed to sell them in our cities. Come join us to…

MARCH FOR OUR LIVES!!!

MARCH FOR OUR LIVES!!!

No Matter How Hard Or How Painful
Or How Much Time it Takes…
We MUST Go the Distance!!!

Meadow Pollack

The Second Amendment provides: A well-regulated militia, being necessary to the security of a free state, the right of the people to keep and bear arms, shall not be infringed. D.C. v Heller, 554 U.S. 570 (2008). In Heller, the U.S. Supreme Court recognized that "the inherent right of self-defense has been central to the Second Amendment" which allows law-abiding, responsible citizens to use arms in defense of hearth and home. It is stated that a law that imposes a severe restriction on the fundamental right of self-defense of the home that it amounts to a destruction of the Second Amendment is unconstitutional under any level of scrutiny.

Here, let's get this out in the open right now and be clear… No American I know is calling for the ban of all firearms here in America. No one I know wants to take away law-abiding, citizens constitutional rights to keep and bear arms, but… everyone I know *does* want stricter gun safety measures put in place, so our kids aren't being massacred in schools and people aren't being mowed down on our streets. That's not too much to ask for. Sure, gun owners don't want their Second Amendment right for self-defense to be infringed upon, but on the same token American's don't want their Fourteenth Amendment right to life, liberty and the pursuit of happiness infringed upon either. Yet, the epidemic of gun violence here in America is infringing on that right.

Again, no one I know is calling to end the Second Amendment. However, we know that like most rights, the right secured by the Second Amendment is not unlimited. From Blackstone through the 19th Century cases, commentators and courts routinely explained that the Second Amendment is "not a right to keep and carry any weapon whatsoever, in any manner whatsoever, and for whatever purpose." Heller, 554 U.S. at 626. The Supreme Court has emphasized that nothing in its recent opinions is intended to cast doubt on the constitutionality of long-standing prohibitions traditionally understood to be outside the scope of the Second Amendment. Importantly, the Second Amendment does not "protect those weapons not typically possessed by law-abiding citizens for lawful purpose". Id. at 625 (citing U.S. v Miller, 307 U.S. 174 (1939). These, longstanding prohibitions on the possession of "dangerous and unusual weapons" have uniformly been recognized as falling outside the scope of the Secord Amendment, Id.; See U.S. v Henry, 688 F.3d 637,640 (9th Cir. 2012) (machine guns are "dangerous and unusual weapons"). Therefore, the gun accessory bump stocks should have never been sold here in America. *Why?* cause it turns a semi-automatic weapon into a "dangerous and unusual" fully automatic machine gun. Our federal government has known this from day one, but again... hasn't cared to ban the sale of them outside of Washington, D.C. *Why?* cause they were getting paid not to do so.

In U.S. v Marzzarella, 614 F.3d, 85 (3d Cir. 2010) the sale of guns with obliterated serial numbers is prohibited, but with these gun show loopholes Americans are able to buy pieces of guns and assemble then later, so again this loophole allows these firearms to be untraceable due to the fact that they now have several serial numbers. In other words, it's like going to a junk yard and taking parts off all different cars in order to make one car. However, all of these firearms go untraceable cause it's not like a car, where you got to register to put on the road at the end of assembly. They simply buy the pieces and assemble them later which completely makes them untraceable. Something we must put an end to. Again, the Law is on our side on this issue. As stated in Justice v Town of Cicero, 577 F.3d 768, 773-74 (7th Cir. 2009) that court ruled that the ordinance requiring the registration of all firearms... appears to be consistent with the United States Supreme Court ruling in Heller. So, the sale of used pieces of weapons that are used to make entire weapons must be banned cause their registration goes completely unregistered. The gun show loopholes and the unvetted background check system allows more than 40 to 50% of all firearms to be sold to unlicensed participants, like criminals and gang members and/or most of these guns are taken and sold for profit on the streets to these same criminals and gang members. For this reason, we must close unvetted loopholes that allow the very people with felony backgrounds to get their hands on these weapons to reign terror on our streets. The crazy part is our federal government and the NRA has known about the loopholes forever and have not cared to do nothing about it. The most ironic part is this is how most of the violent criminals get their guns. *And our government still doesn't care*. Again, the laws are on our side, especially since the Court ruled in U.S. v Williams, 616 F.3d 685, 692-94 (7th Cir. 2010) that all felon criminals are prohibited from ever possessing a firearm. So, *We the People* must close the door on these loopholes. We must demand this in order to prevent these violent criminals from having an unlimited and unvetted supply of weapons. Moreover, the council committee on Public Safety explained: "Registration is critical because it... allows officers to determine in advance whether individuals involved in a call may have firearms and assists law enforcement in determining whether registered owners are eligible to possess firearms, or they have fallen into a prohibited class.

So again, the closure of these gun show loopholes are for the right of public safety. What gets me the most is... *why? Why* aren't law enforcement officers and our federal government a lot more determined to keep the guns off the streets in the first place. I would think that would be one of their main priorities. I would think that law enforcement officials would want to push the federal government into closing the gun show loopholes and properly vetting background checks. I mean... it is for the personal safety of our police officers as well.

Anyhow, while handguns are the most popular weapons chosen by American's for home self-defense purposes, a complete prohibition of their use will fail constitutional muster. But, limiting their magazine size to a standard 10-rounds capacity will save lives and still be acceptable for home self-defense. In doing research, I found that short barreled shotguns are the type of weapon not eligible for Second Amendment protection. And get this... semi-automatic assault rifles are also the type of weapons not eligible for

Secord Amendment Protection. This is how Washington, D.C., is allowed to permanently ban the sale of assault weapons in their state. See Heller v D.C., 670 F.3d 1244. So… while you, me and the kids are trying to push our federal government to implement a ban on all assault weapons around the nation, our federal government has already banned them in their area for the right of their public safety. (Yeah, you just can't trust them!) If it's for their interest – they are with it, but if it's for yours – they are against it. It doesn't make sense, but that's the people that we have elected to make our decisions. In any event, assault weapons should be banned, period. And rightfully so, cause the Council Committee on Public Safety (Committee) also received evidence that assault weapons are not useful for the purposes of sporting or self-defense. They are military-style weapons designed for offensive use. (In other words, their only function is to kill humans). In fact, the Committee concluded that assault weapons 'have no legitimate use as self-defense weapons'. In fact, they increase the danger to law-abiding users and innocent bystanders if kept in the home or used in self-defense situations. Therefore, they literally have no penological purpose being sold on our streets and thus, must be banned. Especially since… assault weapons account for a larger share of guns used in mass murders and the murders of police officers.

The right to possess firearms implies a corresponding right to possess ammunition necessary to use them, but again that right is not unlimited under the Second Amendment. There is (or should be) a prohibition on the possession of large-capacity magazines, which is related to the compelling government interest of public safety. Here is the ugly truth… Washington, D.C. Circuit is the only circuit court to date that has analyzed the constitutionality of a law prohibiting the possession of large-capacity magazines. In its well-reasoned opinion, the court explained that D.C.'s "prohibition of large-capacity round magazines does not effectively disarm individuals or substantially affect their ability to defend themselves." Heller II, 670 F.3d at 1262. The only exception to the ruling is that the only time it's use is permissible is if the lawfully possessed firearm cannot function with a lower capacity magazine, However, there are no guns like that in use and the sale of large-capacity round magazines should be banned all the way across all of the states.

On another note… the manufacture, sole purchase and possession of large-capacity magazines have been regulated in the State of California for approximately twenty years through a combination of federal and state laws. In 1994, Congress enacted the Violent Crime Control and Law Enforcement Act (Crime Control Act) which not only banned assault weapons on the federal level, but also the possession of "large-capacity ammunition feeding devices" – also defined as any magazine capable of accepting more than ten rounds of ammunition which was formerly codified at 18 U.S.C. §922(w); See also San Diego County Gun Rights Comm v. Reno, 98 F.3d. 1121 (9th Cir. 1996).

Beginning in 2000, California criminalized the magazines within the state, but did not specifically criminalize the possession of large-capacity round magazines, which was covered at the time by federal law. See Cal. Penal Code Sections 32310, 16740. But in 2004, the Crime Control Act lapsed leaving the loophole permitting the sale of assault rifles and possession of large-capacity magazines in California.

However, in the wake of recent mass shootings and in recognition of the violence and harm caused by and resulting from both the intentional and accidental misuse of guns, the city of Sunnyvale sought to enhance public safety by enacting further gun safety measures that passed constitutional muster in Fyock v City of Sunnyvale, 779 F.3d 991 (9th Cir. 2015). In the City of Sunnyvale, just like in Washington, D.C., no person may possess a large-capacity magazine whether assembled or dis-assembled and they must surrender their functioning large-capacity magazines to authorities.

In the City of Sunnyvale, they presented evidence that the use of large-capacity magazines results in more gunshots fired, results in more gunshot wounds per victim, and increases the lethality of gunshot injuries. Sunnyvale also presented evidence that large-capacity magazines are disproportionately used in mass shootings as well as crimes against law enforcement. AND... it presented studies that a reduction in the number of larger capacity magazines in circulation may decrease the use of such magazines in gun crimes. Ultimately, the district court found that Sunnyvale submitted pages of credible evidence from study data to expert testimony to the opinions of Sunnyvale public officials, indicating the Sunnyvale ordinance is substantially related to the compelling *government interest in public safety*.

If it wasn't enough, other studies found interest in promoting public safety by limiting large magazine capacity. This was a study conducted by our public officials in, (*yes, none other than*) Washington, D.C. Please see Heller II, 670 F.3d 1244 at 1263-64, that cites study finders that self-defenders of home or hearth using large-capacity magazines are likely to 'keep firing until all bullets have been expended, which poses grave risks to others in the household, passerby and bystanders'.

In other words, the sale of large-capacity round magazines is inherently dangerous to the right of public safety and they too have no penological purpose for self-defense. They have been more harmful than helpful and thus, we must ban the sale of large-capacity magazines capable of accepting more than a standard ten-rounds of ammunition.

We must also implement reasonable waiting periods for the purchases of all firearms. Recently we just saw the State of Florida implement a 3-day waiting period for the purchase of all firearms, but we should demand a minimum of 30 days. In doing so, we can look to California's regulations on the sale and purchase of firearms in the state. Since 1923, the State of California has had some kind of waiting period statue for firearm purchases making the State of Florida is almost 100 years behind in their gun regulations.

In 1955, the California legislature extended the waiting period to 3-days and in 1965 to 5-days. The California Legislative history indicates that the latter change was made to allow sufficient time for California DOJ and law enforcement to complete a background check. The 3-day waiting period was not enough time to run adequate background checks and the 5-day suggested a more useful waiting period. By 1996, the California Legislature extended the waiting period to buy firearms to 15-days and then as the background check system progressed, they brought it down to its current waiting period of 10-days. The California's 10-day waiting period is a reasonable precaution for all purchases of firearms and is presumptively lawful. See Cal. Penal Code Sections 26815 and 27540, For the reasons stated herein, I'm saying Florida's 3-day wait period is not enough time to ensure adequate background checks. Especially in light of the fact that California's 10-day waiting period did not violate the Second Amendment rights of the purchaser. What it did was not only provide sufficient time for law enforcement to complete a background check, but also provided what's known as a "cooling-off period" in which weapons purchasers may reconsider their reasoning for a gun purchase. Particularly when an impulsive act of violence or self-harm maybe contemplated. Also, the law does not violate the Second Amendment rights because the 10-day wait is a reasonable precaution for the purchase of a second or third weapon, as well as for a first purchase. So even to purchase the second or third gun you still have to wait even though you already passed a background check on the first.

For the reasons stated herein, I'm saying first… Florida's 3-day wait period is not enough time to ensure an adequate background check (which the State of California already overwhelming found it was not). Secondly… it doesn't establish a cooling-off period which is a proven method that deters acts of violence to others and one's self. A lot of suicides in our nation is by the use of firearms. By requiring a minimum of a 30-day wait may lead a person to seek mental health treatment from suicidal ideation instead of choosing to blow their brains out. It is also a proven method that helps with random and impulsive acts of violence. The California cooling-off period is set in place to give a person a reasonable chance to stop, think, analyze and respond in an alternative way than violence. Believe it or not, but this happens often where a purchaser will impulsively go to the store in the heat of the moment and legally buy a firearm and use it without getting a real chance to cool-off. A real chance to consult with someone responsible that may talk to them off the latter. *Hey everything is worth a shot.*

The reasons why the NRA doesn't want a 10- to 30-day waiting period (even though this is a proven method that saves lives) is because there are a vast majority of firearms that are purchased impulsively. They obviously do not want a valid waiting period that gives the buyer a chance to rethink his purchase for whatever reason (i.e., no longer thinking irrationally or mad; the kids, the real need for a firearm, etc.). Where otherwise, the purchaser would have bought the firearm. This method is similar to an impulsive gambler that gets locked out of the casino for 30-days. He may have had the urge to surf it out, but he paid his rent that month.

Also, please don't be fooled… our government knows this especially since in Washington, D.C., they already require a person that registered a pistol wait 30-days to register another. The evidence based on this 30-day wait period in D.C. can also be found in the Committee Report that asserts "studies show" that laws restricting multiple purchases or sales of firearms are designed to reduce the number of guns entering the illegal market and to stem the flow of firearms between states 'and that' handguns sold in multiple sales to the same individual purchaser are frequently used in crime. Therefore, we must demand a 30-day waiting period on the sale of all firearms in our nation. Responsible gun purchasers with moral and ethical reasoning would have no problem waiting this 30-days to get a firearm. We should not question our own values when the most important issue at stake here is… life and putting an end to senseless gun violence.

Our greatest objective is to promote public safety by reducing the harm of intention and accidental gun use. This can be done in a series of reasonable measures that do not infringe on a gun purchasers Second Amendment right to the U.S. Constitution and/or infringe on a person's due process rights to life, liberty, and the pursuit of happiness under the Fourteenth Amendment to the Constitution. If making a law-abiding responsible citizen wait 30-days to purchase a firearm save lives, then we owe it to the People of Our Country to implement that, *period*.

Any person that was shot, when it otherwise may have been prevented, was denied their due process right to life and their pursuit of happiness. Kids being scared to go back to school and/or to go to school all around our nation due to the threat of gun violence – *that* – infringes on their right to liberty and freedom to go anywhere they choose. A mom's, a dad's, a brother's, a sister's, a grandparent's, a family member's, and even a friend's pursuit of happiness is also infringed upon every time someone is murdered. It's everyone's worse nightmare come true! So… *We the People* need to get real, if we intend to reduce violent crime and reduce the danger of gun violence. Particularly in the context of shootings, crime against law enforcement, even against suicide. Here, it is evident that our American interest in promoting public safety and ending gun violence is essential. One would think it would be important to our federal governments interest, as well. Well I'll tell you what... I just showed you that it is important to them to protect their home in Washington, D.C., but when it comes to protecting *ours* they are getting paid to look the other way. I keep telling you *they don't care*. So... once again I say... *We the People* must stand up and demand the implementation of our plan! We must...

MARCH FOR OUR LIVES!!!

MARCH FOR OUR LIVES!!!

WE THE PEOPLE MUST Change the Way
Our Politicians MAKE Our Decisions!

Helena Ramsay

*T*o the Federal Politicians… "What's good for the goose IS good for the gander."

When it comes to their public safety, in Washington, D.C., they have enacted every measure to ensure their safety, but when it COMES to yours, mine, and our kids – Our safety is for sale. They have literally, for years, been making poor decisions on one hand and cashing in on the other. They crossed the line in doing so against public safety. Earlier in this book I spoke of treason and that's exactly what it is that they're doing. They are treasonous to us the American People.

If they have a series of laws set in place where they don't sell assault rifles, large-capacity magazines, bump stocks, etc., in Washington, D.C., then there is no way they should allow the sale of them in ours. If they require background checks, eye sight tests, safety training, waiting periods, etc., in our national capital then they should require it all around the nation. Because… "What's good for the goose IS good for the gander".

They have really sold us short by selling us out. We must really take immediate action and change the way our politicians make our decisions for us, cause when they're doing it for money – they're not doing it for us. All else fails if we have no greater ideas. We need to implement a nation-wide gun safety measure similar to those in California. Here in California, they regulate firearm sales and transfers through the Dealer's Record of Sales (DROS) system, which was created a century ago and has been up dated throughout the intervening years. The California DROS system requires that any sale, loan, or transfer of a firearm be made through a licensed dealer (Cal. Penal Code sections 27545, 28050 (a)) requires a dealer to keep standardized computerized record of all such transactions for all purposes. Cal. Penal Code Sections 28100, 23160 et seg,

By making the sale, loan or transfer of all firearms to go through a licensed dealer would instantly close the gun show loopholes that's currently allowing dangerous criminals to get the guns that are being used on our streets to murder us. The statutory framework also requires the California Department of Justice (DOJ) to run background checks prior to purchase, and to notify the dealer if a prospective firearm purchaser is prohibited from possessing a gun under federal laws or under certain provisions of California relating to prior convictions and even mental illness. See Cal. Penal Code Section 28220.

While the DROS system does allow the department to charge a fee of, I believe $19 dollars per firearm purchase (known as a DROS fee) the DROS fee goes to recovering the cost of running these background checks and other related expenses. Cal. Penal Code Section 28225. This fee is also used to fund the DOJ firearm related regulatory and enforcement activities, such as the California Armed Prohibited Persons Systems Program, known as (APPS).

The California APPS program established in 2001, enforces California's prohibition on firearms. This program is for those who, after their legal acquisition of a firearm, later fall into a class of persons who are prohibited from owning or possessing a firearm. This could be due to a felony or violent misdemeanor conviction, domestic violence restraining order, or a mental health related prohibition. Cal. Penal Code Sections 30000, 30005. Essentially, these are people who passed a background check at the time of purchase but no longer pass, yet still possess the firearm The system identifies such people by cross-referencing the Consolidated Firearms Information System (CFIS) database of people who possess a firearm, which is generated primarily through Dealer's Record of Sale reporting, against criminal records, domestic violence restraining order records, and mental health records. Cal. Penal Code Sections 11106, 30005. This process generates a list of armed prohibited persons, which the California Department of Justice uses for investigating, disarming, apprehending, and ensuring the prosecution of persons who have become prohibited from firearm possession.

In simple terminology, this system, if up-dated could be implemented throughout our entire nation. Sure, it would add an additional fee to the gun purchasers, but there is no amount of money that we can put in front of our public safety. If it saves one life, I am sorry about that extra $20 they had to cough up, but we have a kid still here cause of it. If that isn't worth an extra $20... then I don't know... maybe I'm in the wrong country. I thought this was America folks, the most civilized and decent country on the continent. One of the riches countries, as well.

Trust and believe if this Nikolas Cruz had money to purchase 10 guns at the age of 19, he could have purchased 9 and payed the fee that might have gotten us an adequate mental health background check on him that could have prevented this entire freaking heartache. I mean on a National level many firearms are purchased – and I'm sorry – but I'm all for making them pay an extra $5 dollars for a DROS fee, if that added fee would then allow these legal firearm purchasers to come in contact with a trained deputy or firearm expert that may be able to detect a mental health issue that gets us more safety.

I don't know about you, but I'm not trying to meet fate any sooner than I have too and a maniac with a semi-automatic weapon poses a substantial risk to that. So, what if they got to pay an extra one-time fee. They pay a tax into a road safety act every time they pump gas, so every time they buy a firearm they pay a tax into our human safety act. I'm all for it! We just got to get our President and our federal politicians to start making decisions that benefit us and not themselves. They need to align themselves with the views of 70% of the American People, not their pockets. For real... you think I'm playing, but they really need to start making decisions that go to our hearts, not to their wallets. I don't know about you, but I'm tired of that. Those treasonous acts are getting old and if they continue someone really needs to go to jail. So, you know what, in order to get anything closer or better to what I just said, we need to...

MARCH FOR OUR LIVES!!!

WE THE PEOPLE Must Succeed for Our KIDS
Where Our Government Has Failed Us ALL!!

Alex Schachter

You know what, life is not always about where you've been, but where you're going. When I leave this world, I want to make sure I left it in a lot better shape than when I got here. At this point, we have a lot of shaping up to do before then. Right now, that's tackling this gun issue because safety is the first thing we all need next to air, water and food. Without safety and security there is no *US*. At this time, the future of our kids depends on what we do in the present. At this present moment, we have to do more to protect their future and our own.

I don't know about you, but to me our kids are our future and we must invest in them. If it's investing in security to protect their safety, then so be it. Yes, money don't grow on trees, but that's cause we all know it is the tree and there is a lot more where they print them at every day.

Therefore, there is no way we should ever put money over our kid's safety. There is one saying I always loved and I have no clue of who coined it, but it said, "We don't inherent this world from our parents and grandparents, we borrow it from our kids and grandkids". That's why we are borrowing money from our future generations with our 21 Trillion Dollar National Debt. Yes, TODAY many might still be the kids and grandkids, but eventually everyone gets a turn to be the parents and grandparents that many of us already are. Bottom line is we are The People. So, *We the People* have got to band together and do better for our kids TODAY. Here we are trying to protect our kids just so they can get an education. We must stand up to Trump and Congress to get gun reform done. For that, you're either with us or against us, but I'm hoping that you are with us. Because… it's going to take a lot of help to deal with the NRA and the Government. We know that if we wait on Trump and Congress to act on their own accord we aren't going to get much done. History has shown us that by their track record so far on gun control. No longer can we just sit back and wait on their sorry excuse for legislative action. *We the People* must stand up and demand our own action TODAY.

Our kids have already made emotional pleas. So many parents, grandparents, family and friends before them have too and we're still stuck going around and around with these sorry politicians we elected. They don't want to do what we elected them to do and that's make decisions that protect us the American People from foreign and domestic terrorists.

That's why in this book I talked about treason – because really – it's treasonous to go against what the majority of Americans say they want done. In Democracy, the will of the People shall be adhered to and what the majority of us say shall be done, but actually getting our President and Congress to get what we want done hasn't been easy, nor has it been fun. Our governments goal should be to protect our children and ourselves at all cost, but now we know that to them our lives comes with a cost, cause they are selling us out to these lobbyist groups every chance they get. Sorry Bustards! That's why I say… to me, that's treason and to do it for no other reason than money, is really treasonous. *For real*, we pay them really good and they still sell us out for greed, Ungrateful Bustards!!!

Then, look at who their siding against us with, that's what really bugs me the most. While Trump may claim that "The folks who work so hard at the NRA are great people… They love our county and will do the right thing". These are the same People we are fighting against to get adequate gun laws through Congress. They simply don't want to fix the inadequate background checks or even close the gun show loopholes so that dangerous people can't get their paws on the weapons of war. So, the heck with what Trump says, I don't think no one listens to him anyway cause he's on their side. All they're thinking about is the money, they aren't thinking about us! TODAY or any other day either. They would rather not fix the problem than lose money. We don't have the same interests by far because we would rather lose money than lose lives. So, to Trump and the NRA… *boohoo*… cause I really don't care about the billions of bucks they are going to be losing. Right now, the only buck I care about is *why* they keep trying to pass the buck, but I'll tell you what… *the buck stops here.* Right here, right now, *We the People* have to put down our feet and stop this madness, so they won't sell us out… NEVER AGAIN!

Not to mention that Trump and the GOP members of Congress are siding with the NRA.

They're siding with the very ones who are…
Opposed to raising the minimum purchasing age of a firearm to 21.
Opposed to stopping the ban on assault weapons.
Opposed to banning the sale of bump stocks.
Opposed to limiting the large-round capacity round magazines.
Opposed to implementing a cooling-off period.

The NRA, Trump and the GOP Congress are really opposed to everything we want to accomplish when it comes to gun reform. Opposed to everything that we need implemented just to ensure our safety and survival. Passing stricter gun laws is like passing clean air and water rights cause we need them in order to survive. To be honest, I don't know who these people are and where they came from, but one things for sure… *They don't care about us…* the American People. They can say what they want too, but we have kids dying in schools and on the streets AND they don't want to do nothing about it??? yeah right… Let's fire them… I don't even know how we are allowing 5 Million People alleged to be in the NRA to dictate what over 200 Million of us the American People want. I'm sorry but again – *I thought this was a democracy… where the majority rule?* To say the least, there is no way we should stand by and allow them to buy off our politicians to make their idiotic decisions.

That just doesn't make sense, not TODAY, not tomorrow and certainly not even next year. It is a crying shame how it has been permitted to go on for this long. At this point, all our government officials are offering us is – NRA backed modest fixes… When what we need is a major overhaul in this country. The system is broken, and everybody knows it. *We the People* need to demand that they fix it… TODAY. Even they know that everything they have proposed to date – won't work. It's not enough to fix the whole problem.

Trump claimed Nikolas Cruz wouldn't have come into this school if he knew they were armed. However, that defies all rational logic cause Nikolas Cruz attended that school. He knew that MSDHS had an armed resource officer there, and that didn't stop him. I do know we need better security for our kid's safety. The point I was trying to make with that Trump statement is he just talks out the side of his neck and doesn't know what's going on.

Then we turn to the Florida State Government and see that everything that they propose or what little they have done to date is… nothing more than what's considered prescribing an Advil to a cancer patient who's in need of radiation and chemo treatment. As of right now, to use this medical analogy… our gun legislation needs chemo therapy to kill the cancer that's going on with our gun violence epidemic here in America, yet all they want to prescribe is an Advil or Tylenol. Well I'm sorry… *that* is not going to work for our country. A study showed that from just 1991-2014, 160 Million firearms and 15 Million AR-15' s were sold here in America just in that time span. That's not including the 100-150 years before 1991 or the 4 years after 2014. Just from that study, we see that the mass amounts of firearms here in America is astronomical. There are probably more firearms in our homes and on our streets than there are People in our country. Just look, the shooter Nikolas Cruz had 10 firearms himself.

To make a long story short, we literally have to do something other than what we have been doing, which has obviously been *not too much of nothing*. We are in the year 2018 and we don't even have common-sense gun laws on the books OR ones that our federal government care to enforce AND they have allowed the sale, purchase and trade of firearms in America since day one. Then, now we look around at the U.S. and Mexico and see why we have a major gun violence problem in our country. We have allowed almost every criminal in our nation to get their freaking hands on a firearm. Then the real problem is… we don't regulate them like we should. I mean we can sit here and keep talking about this issue until we are blue in the face, but really what we need to do is get red in the face and *do something* about it.

At this point, *We the People* really have to stand up and not only be strong for the fallen, but *We the People* have to stand up and be strong for our kids and ourselves or else we might just be the next fallen victim to gun violence. There is no way that in 2018 we should be sitting here not even talking about it but demanding that our federal government implement common-sense gun safety laws. Common-sense says… 'We should have had that in place since day one'. Now… all of these many years later *We the People* want it, but still can't get it done cause the people who begged us to let them be the ones to help us, have now sold us out. What's the saying "Jimminy-freaking-Christmas".

The crazy part is, do you know what kind of public outcry it would be if manufacturers started making vehicles these days with no air-bags or seat belts? It would be an outcry for real! The heck with that, the world even cried foul when the airbag company Tanaka recently installed faulty airbags in vehicles, let alone could you imagine these days to have none. This is exactly what we're talking about with guns as we have allowed them to sell an unlimited number of guns in our nation without having no real safety procedures set in place and *for that reason* we must cry foul.

I honestly believe that we – the American People – have been crying foul for a long time, but our government has not listened. Over 70% of Americans are saying we want change TODAY and still… we can't get it. SOOO… what we got to do is… vote these Government Officials out. Again… how to vote them all out – **Don't vote for none of the Government Officials that are currently in**

Office! It's just that simple! We just have to get to the point that we are tired of our government's B.S. *We the People* have got to stand up and finally do something about it. Like calling B.S. for what it is… B.S. is B.S. is B.S…. no matter how you look at it. We have to send them a message about the NRA and gun violence like we did with the Big Tobacco companies. Send them the same message… They are allowing us to be killed by these weapons of mass destruction and we are no longer going to stand here silently. I believe the age of the internet and social media has helped in these regards because now people can share their views and opinions with other people all around the world. What we are finding is that a real majority of us, whether Democrat, Republican or Independent… want pretty much the same thing. That's why we have a survey that shows there are 70% in agreement on this particular issue TODAY.

The most bizarre part is more likely than not, 70% are in agreement on every issue I have discussed in this book. It's just a matter of coming together and getting what *We the People* want. For the American People to be in 70% agreement on any issue and not immediately get our request from our government is disturbing. At that rate – they've high-jacked our democracy and turned it into a communistic society and/or like I said, 'They are committing treason against us the American People.'

Now, I could see if 70% of the People wanted crack cocaine, opioid pills or crystal meth off the streets, which that in of itself is a horse of a different color (now that's a different story for another book)! However, for the majority of the People to want stricter gun laws set into place so our kids aren't dying, or our People aren't getting mowed down in the streets, AND our federal government *refuses* to implement that reasonable request cause they are getting paid off… then I'm Sorry… but Houston… *we have a problem.* There is a failure to communicate somewhere along the lines and

I'm going to be the first to say that it is not with us the American People, but with our government. They are really getting paid not to do it and for that reason, somebody should be in trouble. There really are laws for treason. Technically, going against a reasonable request that 70% of the American People have a Constitutional right to, is treasonous to us – the American People.

We really should be demanding somebody be Trumped up on some charges TODAY! The crazy part is... his name just so happens to fit the person we're looking for (TRUMP)!

On that note, all B.S. aside we have to really change our gun laws. We can't keep allowing guns to fall into the hands of dangerous criminals. We have to do more to protect our kids and we have to do more starting TODAY. Therefore, we must stand and demand that we get the necessary stricter gun laws that we need till we win, so until then...

MARCH FOR OUR LIVES!!!

Never Again! We KNOW better,
So... We MUST do better!

Carmen Schentrup

With that said, any of our government officials that abuse their power should be called to accountability. Any of our government officials colluding with the lobbyist against us the American People should be kicked out of power, as well as, any of our government officials that commits treasonous acts against us should be jailed for treason. However, we allow our government officials to do it all, on a consistent basis, and get away with it.

The way I look at it, our government is just as bad, if not worse than Scot Peterson standing at that door, holding that gun and not doing anything to help. We have them somewhere on camera right now literally doing nothing. Seriously, what they need to do is run into that Congress building and use that pen as the mightiest weapon of all and draw us up a complete plan that will keep us safe. NEVER AGAIN already! We have been dealing with gun violence for far too long here in America to not put our feet down now, TODAY!

To be honest, if we don't our feet down now, TODAY, everyone that dies from gun violence is on our hands as well cause we know better, so we must actually do better. If that is demanding that they change gun laws now, TODAY, then we demand that they do it now, TODAY. If that's voting them out cause they don't want to do it, then hey… we already know what we got to do, This is our democracy and *We the People* have to demand that our government meet our demands, or they won't be in that position for very long. The part that gets me the most is that they beg us for it and when we give it to them, they screw us royally. Like… thanks a lot, scumbags!

There is one thing that we can say for sure, everyone knows that we have a gun violence problem here in America. Then, everyone knows that gun ownership comes with grave responsibility, not only on the purchaser but on the seller as well. Therefore, they are fully aware that they have to be more responsible and along with responsibility comes strict rules that everyone must abide by in order to *protect everybody*. All we are asking for is… that everyone do better, period. I mean when we had toys that kids could choke on, what did we do – call for its recall. When we had defective car seats that weren't protecting kids safely, what did we do – call for its recall, When we had toys with lead paint that was shipped from China, what did we do – call for its recall and even when we had defective cribs that our kids had gotten their heads stuck in and/or fell out of, what did we do – call for its recall.

Now we have a violent gun problem with AR-15' s and AK-47's that's being used to mass murder our kids, so what do we do – we call for their recall. We honestly have no other choice, but to do so and you know what? I don't even feel bad because recalling these weapons is a common-sense, no brainer act!

So, to all the men that love their little GI Joe war weapons (it's over)! If the NRA and law-abiding gun owning adults were more responsible, then we wouldn't be having this conversation, but since they have all turned a blind eye and allowed these weapons of war to wind up in the hands of dangerous criminals then… it's not our fault. **We have to do what we have to do as parents to keep our kids safe.** And that is… implement stricter gun laws TODAY. It is extremely out of control! It's time that moms, grandmas, girlfriends and wives take action! Cause obviously… Us grown men can't responsibly control our – not for play – GI Joe toys! This has gone on far too long…

Here – we can go back almost 30-years-ago to Jan. 17, 1989, to the shooting incident that occurred at the Cleveland Elementary School in Stockton, California. While 300 pupils, mostly Kindergartners through third graders, were enjoying their lunch recess, Patrick Purdy, a deranged lunatic, who had placed plugs in his ears to dull the sounds of what he was about to do, drove up to the rear of the school and stepped out of his car carrying a Chinese-made semi-automatic AK-47. "Impassively, Purdy squeezed the trigger of his rifle, then reloaded, raking the yard with at least 106 bullets. As children screamed in pain and fear, Purdy placed a 9mm pistol to his head and killed himself. When the *four-minute* assault was over… five children – ages 6 to 9, were dead. While, one teacher and 29 kids were wounded.

The shooting at the Cleveland Elementary School in Stockton was only one of the terrifying incidents in California involving assault weapons at a school. Five years earlier, in San Ysidro, James Huberty, another psycho drove to a McDonald's restaurant after announcing casually to his wife, "I'm going to hunt humans". On July 18, 1984, Huberty stepped into the restaurant with a 9mm Browning automatic pistol in his belt, along with a 12-gauge shotgun and a 9mm UZI semi-automatic rifle slung over his shoulder and a bag of hundreds of rounds of ammunition. Huberty called out, "Everybody on the Floor". About 50 people were present. As they scrambled to comply, Huberty Marched around the restaurant calmly spraying gunfire.... Maria Diaz ran out the side door in a panic when the shooting started, then remembered that her two-year old son was still inside. She crept back to a window and saw him sitting obediently in a booth. She motioned him toward the door, nudged it open, and the boy toddled to safety. Not everyone was so fortunate. After SWAT sharpshooters finally killed Huberty, police and hospital workers moved in on the gruesome scene. A mother and father lay sprawled across their baby, apparently in an attempt to shield it. All three were dead. The carnage was clearly far worse than it would have been had Huberty not been armed with semi-automatic weapons. He fired hundreds of rounds. The gunfire was so heavy that police at first assumed that more than one gunmen was inside. A fire truck took six shots before reversing direction and backing off. One fire fighter was grazed by a bullet that tore through the truck and then landed softly on his head. In all, of the 50 people in the restaurant, Huberty killed 21 and wounded 19 others.

In 1989, the California Legislature enacted the Roberti-Roos Assault Weapons Control Act imposing restrictions on a class of semi-automatic firearms it characterized as "assault weapons" Cal. Penal Code Section 12275. The restriction was necessary, the

Legislature found and declared, because each of the semi-automatic firearms designated as an assault weapon had "such a high-rate of fire and capacity for the firepower that it's function as a legitimate sports or recreational firearm is substantially outweighed by the danger that it can be used to kill and injure human beings"

At that time the California Legislature stressed, to place restrictions on weapons "primarily designed and intended for hunting, target practice, or other legitimate sports or recreational activities was not its intentions at all, but it was done for the right of public safety because these assault weapons were unlawful human killing machines..."

Moreover, in Kasler v Lockyer (2000) 23 Cal.4th @ 485, Lieutenant Bruce Hagerty, a Los Angeles police officer familiar with gangs and the increasing use of assault weapons, also testified before the Committee of the Whole in 1989-1990, where he stated in part: "Probably the most graphic example, for me, was on Good Friday of last year, where a rival gang entered a neighborhood in South Central Los Angeles and sprayed a crowd of forty to fifty people with an AR-15 and that's an American assault rifle, shooting 14 people, killing a 19 year old boy, hitting a five year old girl, and a 65 year old man, and all ages in between. I was the field commander of that situation, and I'm here to tell you that that was, in every sense of the word, a war scene... There were bodies everywhere and people were terrified, and the only reason that this gang did that was to terrorize the neighborhood because they wanted to take it over and be able to sell drugs in that neighborhood, and the military assault rifle is the vehicle that they used. I'm here to tell you that there's only one reason that they use these weapons, and that is to kill people. They are weapons of war."

In this same case, the then California Attorney General Van de Kamp testified that only the day before testifying, a woman and her unborn child in Los Angeles had been killed by a gang member with an assault weapon. He added: "There was another one down in Lynwood, a nineteen-year-old, who was killed the same day. Increasingly, the weapons of choice for this madness, he noted were semi-automatic military assault rifles". In Los Angeles, he said it had "become fashionable among hard-core members of the Crips gang to spray a stream of bullets in hopes of taking down one rival gang member, but infants and grandmothers may be killed as well. They say that the young killers even have a phrase for it. They say, 'I spray the babies to the eighties'.

Because assault weapons were unregulated, Attorney General Van de Kamp observed, law enforcement officials did not know how many of them were on the streets of California. However, he added, ''we do know that the numbers are going up at a frightening rate. Hard hit police departments have begun to keep records, like Oakland, California, where the number seized has tripled in less than two years. Statewide, the number of semi-automatic weapons seized – by law enforcement has more than doubled in the last two years. A partially completed Department of Justice survey with 132 law enforcement agencies reporting thus far has found the same pattern for semi-automatic weapons used in crimes. The number has doubled in the last two years, the number used in shootings has gone up nearly 300. Clearly, we are "seeing an escalation in the arms race, and law enforcement is losing".

These are just a few cases I did a little research on, a needle in the hay stack to the vast amount of gun violence cases that we have faced in our nation. I mean all of the above occurred over 29+ years ago. So really, that's why I referenced these cases in here is because our government has known about the escalation of assault weapons and how they have wreaked communities in our country for decades. Yet, they still stand by TODAY and do nothing to stop the madness that I just referenced. It has gone on for far too long, to just say the least. Even till this day, we are talking about another massacre at the MSDHS where 17 kids and teachers were shot and killed. 15 others wounded. Then in Oct. of 2017, we had the Las Vegas massacre with 58 dead and over 500 wounded. I can keep going on forever it seems like. Where do we as the American People draw the line in the sand and tell our federal government they are wrong as two left shoes for failing to implement strict gun laws TODAY.

We don't even need to look at the Sandy Hook's, the Virginia Tech's or even the Columbine High School shooting that occurred almost 20 years ago to see that nothing has changed. During the Clinton era, the Democrats put their foot down and banned assault weapons in our nation, but that only lasted from 1994 to 2004, and then W. Bush, and the then GOP were paid off by the NRA and gun lobbyist corporations to not reimplement the assault weapons ban. Here we sit TODAY, in the same or worse position than we were in 30 years ago and now it's time *We the People* stand up and put this gun violence to an end...

MARCH FOR OUR LIVES!!!

MARCH FOR OUR LIVES!!!

Yes... One Single Thing Will NOT work,
But a Combination of Things WILL...

Peter Wang

Here we've seen President Trump hold listening sessions at the White House in the wake of this MSDHS shooting with students, parents and teachers from previous mass shootings. But... if he was actually listening he would have heard that they all (and we all) want him to implement major gun reform now. As of TODAY, I can say either he wasn't listening, didn't take us seriously and/or simply didn't care to do anything, cause he has only talked in circles about everything he was talking about. To say the least, he has done nothing we asked him to do. I would have thought that in wake of the mass gun violence going on in our country they would have done major gun reform in using the term "lickety-split", but now I don't even think they plan on doing it in a lifetime. I honestly sit here and I'm not kidding you, it makes me think our government officials are on some kind of hallucinogen cause they really got to be hallucinating to think we are going away. Gun violence is not going away and we're not going away either until they totally fix this damn problem.

We have moms demanding action, dads demanding action, kids demanding action, grandparents demanding action and over 70% of the American People demanding action, so we are not going away. The fact that they have gotten nothing done as of me writing this TODAY, just proves that they have no understanding, compassion or empathy for us the American People in any way. Then, you have People like Laura Ingraham on Fox News claiming: "The NRA does more to promote gun safety than any other organizations in America but even if on paper they did more, ..." which to me is fake news and a crock of crap because they can spin it however they want too, and we still come back around to the fact that they share no view points on gun reform that the 70% of Americans share. This organization has been paying our politicians to look the other way for years. These people are real crooks and hearing her defend these scumbags when we have People dying by gun violence by the hundreds is just another slap in the face or a punch in the gut by yet another punch-drunk GOP Republican. She needs to leave that punch alone cause she even talks like a drunk, *for real!*

I honestly don't know what more to say, especially since I got to get this book out by the end of the day. Besides, I believe our message here is loud and clear. We can never do enough, if we care enough – and I'm pretty sure we all do – so from me to you, please let's do what it takes and hopefully we can get it done even if Donald Trump and the GOP Republican's flake. You know what, when the going gets tuff, the tuff gets going and the crazy part is you never know how tuff you got to be until being tuff is your only option.

At this point, being tuff is our only option! *We the* People have got to really fight Trump, Congress and the NRA to get us the necessary gun law reform we need TODAY. The benefits of our fight will definitely outweigh the cost. The costs we lose is human lives and we can't afford any more of that (if we ever could at all). They should have fixed these gun laws years ago, and if they don't now, another mass shooting will be all their fault, I talked about knowing better and doing better, so I know they know better, I just hope they do better!

Our politicians are always talking about sides, but they need to leave all the politic rhetoric outside the door cause this gun issue has no side. It effects everyone. Besides, none of their decisions should be for political reasons anyway, they should always make them with the best interest of the American People. Here, our President had another opportunity to bring us together and he has once again drawn the line in the sand against us... for money. He has failed miserably and should be ashamed cause this was the time to grab your kids and hug them, pull them close and tell them that you love them, but he didn't try to console the kids or the families... he didn't even show up to these kids CNN Town Hall Meeting. I would have thought that he would have shown more maturity and showed that he cared. Obviously, he didn't care as he was seen playing golf instead. And what about the tweets that he shared, nope... no caring there either.

However, the heck with Trump, together we stand and no matter what... *We the People* will eventually win in the end. We even went to Washington, D.C. already and had a lay-in, where 17 teens participated for the 17 that were killed at MSDHS, and we still haven't got nothing done. What about the March… nope still nothing. If it takes wisdom and courage to pursue change, then we have it all, we are smarter, we are stronger, and we will fight through it all. Like the MSDHS "SHINE" song says, "You may have brought the dark, but together we will shine the light". We must fight cause if we don't – our life – could be the next one we lose by gun violence.

There is no rest for the weary, there shall be no faint of heart, we the American People have been strong from the start. At this time, we are just in another tug of war with our politicians and we must win. If we are to pull, I will tell you to pull harder, give it all you got and whatever you do please don't give out. We are in a life or death struggle and we must not give out. Like Harry S. Truman said "We are going to fight hard, we are going to give them hell" cause whenever the American People are called upon, we always answer the bell. This time it's no different. *What did they think?* We are going to just go away, yeah like I said earlier, not TODAY!

We shall turn our grief into action, cause we refuse to go back to our lives and classrooms empty handed. We will not kick back, we shall kick it into gear, we will not lag behind, we will be like the MSDHS kids and win the State Hockey Championship Title in a landslide. Every year on February 14th at 3pm we will be standing there with our hands over our hearts of those that we loved and lost herein.

Well like Frederick Langbridge said: "Two men look through the same bars, one sees mud, and one see stars", so all I can say is keep your head up and look to the stars, they called these kids crisis actors cause they were really smart and that's why I know they will go very far. They say when life gives you lemons, make lemonade and I'll tell you if you find yourself in a not so cool position, make Kool-Aid. I'll tell you this last thing before I go, whatever you do in life I hope you don't lose. I will just tell you like the MSDHS kid said, don't forget to "eat the cake and buy the shoes". Other than that, we are going to stand up and…

March till we win,
cause you know what???
Never Again!

MARCH FOR OUR LIVES!!!
***
COMMON-SENSE GUN REFORM LAWS

I'M CALLING ON OUR FEDERAL GOVERNMENT TO:

1) Ban the sale, loan, transfer and trade in the U.S. of all assault weapons *just like they are already banned in Washington, D.C.,* under Heller v D.C., 670 F.3d 1244.

2) Ban the sale, loan, transfer and trade in the U.S. of all large-capacity magazines capable of accepting more than 10-rounds of ammunition *just like they are already banned in Washington, D.C.,* under Heller v D.C., 670 F.3d 1244; and/or fully ban the receipt in the U.S. of all large-capacity magazines capable of accepting more than 10-rounds of ammunition *just like they are already banned in the City of Sunnyvale, California,* under Fyock v City of Sunnyvale, 779 F.3d 991 (2015).

3) Ban the sale, loan, transfer, and trade in the U.S. of all bump stock accessories which illegally turns a semi-automatic

assault weapon into a fully-automatic machine gun *just like they are already banned in Washington, D.C.,* under Heller v D.C., 670 F.3d 1244; see also U.S. v Henry, 688 F.3d 637, 640 (9th Cir. 2012) ("Machine guns are dangerous and unusual weapons").

4) Ban the sale, loan, transfer and trade in the U.S. of all new or used firearm (parts) which can later be pieced together and assembled to make unregistered firearms under U.S. Marzzarella, 614 F.3d 85 (3rd Cir. 2010); Justice v Town of Cicero, 577 F.3d 768, 773-74 (7th Cir. 2009).

5) Raise the minimum purchasing age in the U.S. on all firearms to the age of 21.

6) Limit the sale in the U.S. to (2) firearms (1 Handgun and 1 Rifle) to anyone under the age of 25 (Based on scientific evidence that a youth's brain is not fully developed till the age of 25) under Miller v Alabama, 132 S.Ct. 2455 (2012); Graham v Florida, 56 U.S. 48, 75 (2010); Roper v Simmons (2005) 543 U.S. 551; see also People v Franklin, 63 Cal.4th 261 (2016).

7) Limit the sale in the U.S. to a maximum of (7) firearms to anyone over the age of 25. (This will limit the purchase of legally purchased firearms being sold on the black market to domestic terrorists by unlawful abiding citizens)! Besides, 300 Million People x 7 Firearms per person equals 2.1

Billion Firearms in the U.S. alone... How many more guns do we need? There must be a limit of how many firearms one person can purchase and once they reach that limit we offer a one-for-one exchange.

8) Limit the register in the U.S. of all firearms to (1) per 30-days *just like they did in Washington, D.C.,* under Heller v D.C., 670 F.3d 1244.

9) Establish a strict 30-day waiting period in the U.S. for all firearms sold, loaned, transferred or traded in order to conduct a reasonable background check and it will give a person an adequate cooling-off period. (i.e., impulsive acts of violence and/or suicidal self-harm)! *Which is similar to the State of California's 10-day cooling off period* under Cal. Penal Code Sections 26815 and 27540.

10) Establish a Universal Dealer's Record of Sales (DROS) System in the U. S. in order to conduct extensive background vetting checks, *that is equal to or greater than the one implemented in the State of California* under Cal. Penal code Sections 27545, 28050(a), and 28225.

11) Establish a Universal Consolidated Firearm Information System (CFIS) Database in the U.S. that must be mandatorily updated by each State, *that is equal to or greater than the one implemented in the State of California* Under Cal. Penal Code Sections 11106 and 30005.

12) Close all gun show loopholes by mandatorily requiring everyone in the U.S. to buy, sell, loan, transfer and trade all firearms, bullets and accessories through the updated (DROS) System and (CFIS) Database.

13) Establish a Universal Armed Prohibited Persons Systems Program (APPS) System in the U.S. that will enforce the rule of law that criminals must not have firearms, *that is equal to or greater than the one implemented in the State of California* under Cal. Penal Code Sections 30000, 30005.

14) Establish a Universal Red Flag System (RFS) in the U.S. that gives the police authority to temporarily confiscate a person's firearms when they're appearing to be mentally unstable or emotionally distraught. (i.e., If they say they are going to harm someone or themselves, joking or not, take it)!

15) Establish a Universal Registration Requirement System (RRS) in the U.S. that requires both parties that are either buying, selling, loaning, transferring, trading, and/or registering a firearm (unless purchased new) to:

   a. Appear in person with the unloaded firearm
   b. Disclose all information:
      i. Full legal name
      ii. Address
      iii. Valid government issued photo ID
      iv. Social Security Number

      v. Occupation

      vi. Current place of employment

      vii. All previous documentation about the firearm

  c. Disclose bullet information

  d. Submit to a fingerprint and photograph

  e. Pass background check

  f. Pass mental health exam

  g. Pass vision requirements

  h. Pass a firearm training and safety course

      i. Total of at least 1-hour of firing

      ii. Total of 4-hours safety training

  i. Submit to mandatory random check-ups on firearms;

  j. Notify authorities within 24-Hours if their firearm is lost, missing or stolen

  k. Sign a letter of agreement that they have read and understand all rules and regulations of owning a firearm and penalties thereof for breaking any of the laws.

16) I am also requesting that they implement active shooting drills at all schools in the U.S. *that is equal to or greater than all fire and earth quake drills.*

17) Establish a Universal School Officer Security (SOS) "Save Our Students" System in the U.S., where each school will have a minimum of one Officer or Military Personnel per 1000 Students. Then, implement a (secure) firearm safety storage unit in a (secure) designated office on campus that contains the necessary hardware (i.e., firearms, bulletproof vests and/or bulletproof shield) that all school officer's and (only) required trained school faculty have access to in case of emergency. (To personally allow school faculty to carry concealed weapons on their person as Trump stated, *'oh… heck no!!!'*) I only say the later because it will harden the school's thinking beyond having school officer's. Allowing (properly) trained school faculty to have access to a firearm and a reasonable way to protect themselves with a bullet proof vest would only be in an emergency situation! With this later idea, I know one would think about all the what if's (i.e., someone getting a hold of the firearms in the (secure) safety storage unit… and using them against us?) If that happens then honestly, we are at a sad day because we are already dealing with a mentally deranged individual at that point! As a dad, I can live with that, I think!

With that said, these are the (17) Common-sense Gun Reform laws that I'm proposing, which just so happens to be a law for each of the 17 students that died at the MSDHS shooting. in order to keep our students and ourselves safe. Don't ask me, it just came out that way! It is my greatest hope that our President and Congress act on our behalf in passing stricter Gun reform measures that would only help to keep ourselves and our communities safer.

To the Survivors, Parents. Families and Friends affected by the Marjory Stoneman Douglas High School Shooting, also to those in all the other mass shootings as well that have came before this book and those that will come after, and also to all those around the globe affected by Gun violence. "I'm Sorry!" I know the kids at MSDHS said they didn't want thoughts and prayers, they wanted action! I can only say that I've done my best to call our Government and our American People into action. I can only pray that my thoughts and prayers at this point, will *please*... be received. If I had the authority to act on implementing the above laws, and/or if I heard any other great ideas to go along with them, I promise you I would not hesitate to implement anything that I thought would work quick, fast and in a hurry... TODAY.

Hence, I'm Sorry!... No Parent, Student, Teacher, Friend, Family Member and/or Pet, should have to go without the spirit of the loved one that made them happy and brought them warmth inside. With that... I would like to send out my most heartfelt thoughts. prayers and condolences to all those affected by gun violence around the planet. May you find peace, may you find the will to survive, and may you – for what it is worth – find the will power to keep hope alive. All I can possibly say is... *keep one foot in front of in front of the other headed towards God's Glory* and Once Again "I'm Sorry"!

To America... We are the land of the free and the home of the brave! Dammit, let's show them what we're made of!

LET'S GOOOO!!!

BAN ASSAULT WEAPONS AND CHANGE GUN LAWS
NOW!
***
IF IT'S ONLY:
"Necessary for the Good Man to do Nothing
For Evil to Triumph."

-Edmund Burke

Then please don't be the SCOT PETERSON'S of the world…
or the DONALD TRUMPS!

AGAIN:
If the Good Man Did Nothing In the Face of Evil
He Wasn't a GOOD MAN to Begin With… For Real!!!

SO PLEASE:
Don't Be the One to Do Nothing…
Be BRAVE, COURAGEOUS, DARING...
Be the EVIL KNIVEL!

THEREFORE, IF YOUR WITH US:
PLEASE Be With Us Till We WIN...
CAUSE WE CAN'T PUT UP WITH THIS GUN VIOLENCE
ANYMORE!!!
NEVER AGAIN!

MARCH FOR OUR LIVES!!!

OMG

THE END!!!

P.S. Thank you for letting me rant and rave…
And thankyou to everyone helping make a change, Smile!

***

P.S.S. TO DONALD TRUMP AND CONGRESS:

STOP BEING FREAKING TURDS,

STAND UP TO THE NRA AND BE A VERB!

OMG!!!

COMING SOON:

ENOUGH IS ENOUGH

PROLOGUE

***

Enough
-Is-
Enough!

***

WELCOME TO THE REVOLUTION

WE WON'T NEVER GIVE UP…

STAND UP AMERICA!!!

OUR LIVES ARE BEING ROBBED!

FIGHT FOR YOUR LIVES

BEFORE… IT'S SOMEONE ELSE'S JOB…

OMG

A MUST READ!!!

***

THIS BOOK IS WRITTEN TO ACKNOWLEDGE ALL THOSE AFFECTED

BY GUN VIOLENCE HERE IN AMERICA

AND AROUND THE GLOBE…

"I'M SORRY"!!!

WE FAILED YOU!

HOWEVER:

WE WILL PREVAIL WHERE WE HAVE FAILED

ARE YOU STILL WITH US OR WHAT???

BECAUSE:

HE WHO ACCEPTS EVIL

WITHOUT PROTESTING AGAINST IT IS…

REALLY COOPERATING WITH IT!

-DR. MARTIN LUTHER KING, JR.,

LIKE THEY SAY:

IF YOU'RE NOT PART OF THE SOLUTION

THEN YOU'RE PART OF THE PROBLEM!!!

LIKE I'LL SAY:

IF CONGRESS DON'T WANT TO DO NOTHING –

TO SOLVE OUR GUN VIOLENCE PROBLEM

THEN THEY'RE ONLY PERPETUATING ITS EXISTENCE

WHICH IS REALLY COOPERATING WITH IT!!!

-ELLIOTT LEW GRIFFIN

I'M MARCHING WITH THE KIDS:

IF CONGRESS SITS BACK AND DOES NOTHING

WHILE THE SHIT HITS THE FAN, THEN YES,

THEY DO "HAVE BLOOD ON THEIR HANDS"!!!

-MSDHS

OMG

***

LET ME MAKE ONE THING CLEAR FOR STARTERS HERE:

WE DON'T GIVE:

NOT A

RATS

ASS

ABOUT THE NRA!!!

That's for sure! Trust and believe I'm not a kid and no one from the left is manipulating me into writing this. The billionaires aren't paying me and I'm far from a Hollywood success. So... to the NRA and want to be Conservative hard-liners alike... you can please save your unsympathetic immature comments towards these kids to *yourself*!!! These kids are victims of a horrific unimaginable tragedy and have (every) right to gripe about what's going on in our country. These kids should never have been personally attacked or criticized for what they had to say. Not TODAY, not tomorrow and definitely not yesterday. If anything, everything that they have said should have been elevated... in a special kind of way...

To be honest... none of these Marjory Stoneman Douglas High School (MSDHS) kids have outright called for a repeal of the Second Amendment. So... the NRA can save their lying rhetoric cause nobody's buying it. Yes... these kids, their friends and families are grieving, but their call for sensible gun laws in the wake of this gun violence epidemic in our country is far from venting. Especially, since the majority of the American People (70%) agree with them on the many talked about, REAL issues. That's why I say the leaders of the NRA can save their stupid fuss... cause really... they're just mad that their NRA hush money is not going to work on us anymore. One thing for sure, if they don't have nothing nice to say to these kids... then **I and probably everyone else...** would appreciate that they say nothing at all. Their comments and personal attacks on these kids aren't making this issue any better. Especially, since I truly believe they are the:

NITWITS
RUINING
AMERICA

SO… TAKE THAT NRA…
AND LEAVE THESE KIDS ALONE!

***

Enough is Enough!

***

CHAPTER 1

DID YOU SEE OUR KIDS

MARCH FOR OUR LIVES!

You know what we do know? Is united we live, divided we die and that's why on March 24, 2018 we had over 800 rallies world-wide for "MARCH FOR OUR LIVES". We had millions of people rally around our kids from MSDHS, along with many other survivors of gun violence from around the world. Whether you Marched, watched (or not), we still Marched and watched for you, *Why?* Because, believe it or not… *bullets don't discriminate.* So, this issue of gun violence, whichever side of the isle you're on, still affects you, *please* believe it!

If you did miss it, it was impressive! I'm so proud of our kids and all of the participants. It was the biggest March in modern day history, where it was estimated that roughly 800,000 people alone gathered to March from the U.S. Capital to the White House in Washington, D.C. I wasn't there, but on TV it was a site to be seen. Then not to mention, the massive crowds that rallied from coast to coast, sea to shining sea, and nation to nation for common-sense gun reform. One thing I know for sure is that we have so many strong people around the world that I know we will overcome gun violence here in America and around the globe.

It was amazing to see so many people come together around the world that I honestly don't know where to start, but I will say that the revolution to end gun violence is definitely underway. It's like I heard my baby daughter say many of times "we're going to turn it up" and she's 14. Little does she know is that her dad's generation invented that and that we're with it till the end… We're gonna turn it all the way up to 10. Then we're even going to put on the Lil John song "Turn it down for what?" Except we will do it for Emma Gonzalez cause it was her silence at the March for our Lives rally that truly spoke volumes. It really gets no louder than that!!! She turned it up to 11.

We are the generation that has the power to drastically damper gun violence here in America and we must continue to come together in order to achieve that goal. I saw all of the signs that the people were displaying around globe and the one that struck me the most was a little girl holding a sign that said, "I am 6, so were they. NEVER AGAIN" in reference to the kids we lost in the Sandy Hook Elementary School massacre in Newtown, CT. Yet after seeing that sign and many others we still can't even get Congress to act responsibly right now. To say the least, it's a sad sight for poor eyes. The day before the Marches began, Congress passed what's known as the "Fix Nics" bill which only mildly strengthened the background check system and the Stop School Violence Act in which a Committee is set to *come up with school safety measures*. Then Congress and the Department of Justice (DOJ) set out to ban the gun accessory known as "Bump Stocks" which illegally turned a semi-automatic assault weapon into a fully automatic machine gun, but that won't take effect for 90 days.

HOWEVER… all of it is a *hoax*! Without Congress implementing Universal background checks… we still have *no gun reform whatsoever*. Even if we were to put the background check system in the background, without Congress closing the gun show loopholes, we are still left with no gun reform whatsoever. Then the Stop School Violence Act sounds good... but that too is a *hoax*. Congress can't even come up with the right measures to prevent the bad guys from getting the guns in the first place, so to rely on them to come up with common-sense measures that will ensure school safety is... in my opinion... not going to happen. And... whatever they do come up with, I can sadly assure you that the *devil* will be in the details. I always say that anything short of **brave** armed guards or soldiers watching over our kids at school is complete buffoonery. Then after that without no gun prevention laws implemented what are we expected to do with everything else.

This Trump administration has continuedly called for the personal arming of teachers, but like the MSDHS kid said: "What are we going to do after that... arm our preachers, pastors and Rabbi's. The ticket man at the movie theater?" Nothing of what this Trump administration has come up with so far or implemented to date has made any sense. For Congress and the White House to even pass bills like these, I'm left with only the thought that they don't even have sense, let alone common-sense. If they do have any sense it's evident that they're not using it to save our lives, but rather to keep the cents going on their bottom lines. Especially since they may have well as did nothing. Since the "Fix Nic's" bill literally did nothing!

Then the most bizarre part is that Congress and the DOJ set out to ban bump stocks, but they did us no favor cause they didn't ban the sale of them starting that day. TODAY, they are still on the market for sale in our nation. I guess they intend for them to completely sell out of stock before they ban them entirely. They had since October 2, 2017 the day after the Las Vegas Massacre to do this. Now I'm sure somewhere on some website they have a going out of manufacturer sale on them where they are on sale for half price. Or at a buy one get two free offer. Right now, as we speak, they're selling off the shelves like hotcakes. To be honest… these people are so crazy that they probably raised the price to triple their value. Since they now know the last remaining bump stocks in stock are a rare commodity that they won't ever be sold again in America. Then for a president that swears he doesn't telegraph what he is going to do, he telegraphed that he was going to stop the sale of bump stocks. Maybe that was the dog whistle to get out and buy now so they can forever hold onto their bump stock piece.

Wow… is all I can say! Our President and Congress are to be of our best and brightest minds, but I'm sad to report that they literally have to be of the most-dumbest that we can find at this time! If they really think that what tiny modifications they did was going to prevent, let alone stop, the gun violence in America, they are sadly mistaken. Then again, maybe it is *We the People* that are sadly mistaken to think that our federal government was going to fix it.

Not to mention, what our former Senator Rick Santorum had said to these kids, and basically to all of us, cause we were at the rallies as well, in that we all need to take CPR classes instead of looking for someone to solve our problems. To be honest I was stunned and felt dumbfounded when he said that. Then laughed when the lady on CNN said, "and that's why he's our *former* senator". (Ha-ha) I got a kick out of that. I couldn't have said it better myself and I'm pretty good coming up with retorts to those kinds of things. Now I'm back looking around and thinking (I see why we're at where we're at) after having someone like him in Congress. Just think, I even believe he was trying to throw his hat in the ring to be president too. Then again, I highly doubt it gets much worse than Trump anyways. Rick Santorum's statements should come as no surprise given the fact that Donald Trump must be thinking as much, if not worse about us and these kids. Especially since he has flip-flopped on this issue already and then hasn't done anything to cure it either. To tell you the truth, I don't even expect him too. I thought Congress would do something more given it's a mid-term election year. You would think that they would want to keep their jobs but passing a 1.3 Trillion-dollar spending bill that we're footing with very minimal gun reform legislation is not going to cut it this year. I honestly thought they knew that. I guess that was before they witnessed the world-wide March for our Lives rallies. I hope that vision puts a little 'ants in their pants' to do something. If not, then we know what we got to do...

What more can I say at this point but to give you a quote from the Bible:

"TO EVERYTHING THERE IS A SEASON, AND A TIME TO EVERY PURPOSE UNDER THE HEAVEN:
A TIME TO BE BORN AND A TIME TO DIE; A TIME TO PLANT AND A TIME TO PLUCK UP THAT WHICH IS PLANTED;
A TIME TO KILL AND A TIME TO HEAL; A TIME TO BREAKDOWN AND A TIME TO BUILD UP;
A TIME TO WEEP AND A TIME TO LAUGH; A TIME TO MOURN AND A TIME TO DANCE;
A TIME TO CAST AWAY STONES AND A TIME TO GATHER STONES TOGETHER; A TIME TO EMBRACE AND A TIME TO REFRAIN FROM EMBRACING;
A TIME TO GET AND A TIME TO LOSE; A TIME TO KEEP AND A TIME TO CAST AWAY;
A TIME TO REND AND A TIME TO SOW; A TIME TO KEEP SILENCE AND A TIME TO SPEAK; AND
A TIME TO LOVE AND A TIME TO HATE; A TIME FOR WAR AND A TIME FOR PEACE.
-Bible, Ecclesiastes 3: 1-8

I'll tell you what, it's a time that we put an end to gun violence and it's a time that we change our government. So, if you're tired of our government's chaos, confusion, madness and fuss, then I beg you to please jump on board this March to end gun violence with us because… we are going to change our government in the process too.

ENOUGH IS ENOUGH!

OMG

A MUST READ

www.ingramcontent.com/pod-product-compliance
Lightning Source LLC
Chambersburg PA
CBHW062159280526
45788CB00001B/362